MEMORIES OF BEN HILL DRIVE

A SOUTHERN STORY

Hubert F. Addleton

A Note on the Cover Art

The cover drawing of our old family home on Ben Hill Drive (since demolished) was done as a 90th birthday present by one of my granddaughters, Alexandra (Alec) Addleton. She is an accomplished professional artist who lives and works in Atlanta.

Doorlight Publications
www.doorlightpublications.com

Copyright ©2019 Hubert F Addleton
Cover Art ©2019 Alexandra Addleton

All rights reserved. No part of this book may be reproduced in any form, except as permitted by US copyright laws, without written permission from Doorlight Publications.
First published 2019 by Doorlight Publications.

ISBN   0-9982233-4-4
ISBN13 978-0-9982233-4-6

Design & Production by Ruth Anne Burke

Write down for the coming generations
What the Lord has done,
So that people not yet born
Will praise him.

Psalms 102:19

And some there be, which hath no memorial;
Who are perished, as though they had never been;
And are become as though they had never been born;
And their children after them.
But these were merciful men,
Whose righteousness hath not been forgotten.

Their bodies are buried in peace;
But their name liveth for evermore.
The people will tell of their wisdom,
And the congregation will shew forth their praise.

Ecclesiasticus 44:9

CONTENTS

Foreword	v
1. Ben Hill Drive	1
2. Papa and Mama	17
3. Brothers and Sisters	31
4. Calling	51
5. Pakistan	61
Photos	73
Acknowledgments	103
Appendix A: Education History	105
Appendix B: Pastorates	106
Appendix C: Work History	107
Appendix D: Countries Visited	109
Appendix E: Genealogy	110
About the Author	115

Foreword
by Jonathan Addleton:

Dad's memories provided in the pages that follow offer an important perspective on Macon, Ben Hill Drive, Addleton family history – and the dynamics of childhood and community life in a changing American South and beyond.

Perhaps inadvertently, Dad's reflections also became the catalyst for further introspection on my part. Just as Dad looks back with wonder on his Middle Georgia childhood and later service as a Baptist missionary in Pakistan, I too am astonished at the forces that shaped my childhood in Pakistan and then propelled me to a lifetime of secular service as a diplomat involving eleven countries on four continents.

Did my background as the son of missionary parents from rural Middle Georgia compel me along a path that ultimately led to a 32-year Foreign Service career, one that eventually included assignments as US Ambassador to Mongolia, USAID Representative to the European Union and USAID country director in India, Pakistan, Cambodia and Central Asia? Did my faith, shaped partly but not completely by my parents, make a difference? Or was this career choice part of a much longer journey, one that did not begin with my entry into the world but was also connected to the decisions made by my parents and their parents before them?

Looking at the circumstances of Dad's upbringing, I can't help but superimpose his family into some of the iconic photos depicting the realities of the Great Depression, especially those taken in the rural American South showing large families with barefoot children standing outside their tar paper shacks not unlike the drafty plank house on Graham Road in Jones County where Dad spent the first ten years of his life. As he relates in these pages, he felt "embarrassed" when he later took the bus to Alexander III elementary school in Macon, arriving on that first day barefoot and without shoes.

In retrospect, there is a clear demarcation between the older siblings in the Addleton family who came of age during the Great Depression and faced harsh economic realities and the younger siblings who received more education and had more opportunities open to them. Dad benefitted in that he was able to continue in school and did not have to follow his older brothers and sisters into the cotton mills.

President Roosevelt also made a difference. Like so many others at the time, the Addleton family grew up revering him, listening to his occasional "fireside chats" on the radio affirming that people like them actually mattered. Roosevelt's visits to swim with other polio patients in the therapeutic waters of Warm Springs between Macon and Columbus added to his mystique. World War II also made a difference, expanding horizons and opening up a wider world beyond Middle Georgia.

Dad was born in November 1929, two years too late to fight in World War II though some of his older brothers served. However, his life prospects changed dramatically after the war, allowing him to fulfill an early compulsion to complete high school, enroll in Bible School, attend seminary and eventually become a missionary, fulfilling his true calling. As related in this manuscript, in 1956, at the age of 26, he departed from New York for Pakistan on a World War II era freighter named the *Steel King,* accompanied by his wife and young son – my older brother David.

During that first assignment in Pakistan Mom and Dad had two more children: I was born in 1957 in Murree and my sister Nancy followed two years later. Both of us were born at Rock Edge, a small collection of summer vacation homes situated in the foothills of the Himalayas with a stunning view toward Kashmir.

During the 34 years that Dad spent in Pakistan he helped found a small school for the children of Christian sweepers in Jacobabad, played a part in establishing a hospital for women in Shikarpur, worked in both Shikarpur and Hyderabad to translate the four Gospels into the Sindhi language and organized an international congregation in Pakistan's largest city, Karachi.

Throughout those years he worked closely with the small and impoverished Pakistani Christian community while also bearing witness to his faith among the Muslims that surrounded him, forging life-long friendships along the way.

Financial support was provided by individual churches throughout America offering modest contributions, one in a coal mining town in western Virginia, another in rural Mississippi, a third located as far away as Mariposa, California. Every fifth year our parents returned to the United States to report back on what they had accomplished.

During these years my parents raised three children in a remote corner of southern Pakistan, the middle one of which became me. Their early choices ultimately shaped my own, including my decision to join the Foreign Service and embark on a USAID career.

Perhaps some of those early memories from Pakistan -- pastoral visits in the slums of Shikarpur, funerals for infants who died much too young, surviving adolescents scarred for life with small pox – helped frame much of my later life, firmly pointing me toward a development career.

Looking back, the journey taken by the Addleton family over the last century helps highlight some of the many factors that can make a difference in individual lives as well as in entire societies:

Family Matters: As a university student I learned that classical economics is built on rational decisions made by individuals acting alone. In real life I became aware that for many the family is a far more compelling focus of interest and analysis.

Growing up in Pakistan I saw families make hard choices – this child is smart, we should sacrifice to give him a better future; that child has nimble fingers, she is the one who should weave carpets so her brother can go to school.

Strong families also support each other throughout a lifetime, as my father experienced growing up in the Depression era American South. For more than seventy years, the extended Addleton family has gathered every year on the last Saturday before Christmas to remember their parents, celebrate together and recall their heritage.

Faith Matters: The role of faith in transforming lives is rarely talked about, at least in Foreign Service circles where I spent much of my working life. Yet it undeniably plays a role. Growing up in the Great Depression during the 1930s, the Addletons were not a church-going family. But something happened during the 1930s and in the Willingham Mill Village and especially at Willingham Baptist Church that changed everything.

A few years ago I attended a "homecoming" at that church, the sanctuary filled with the second and third generation of families whose parents and grandparents had worked in the cotton mills, typically from an early age.

Three of Dad's brothers are also part of this spiritual story, having become Baptist or Pentecostal preachers. Two of them attended the same college in Mississippi, an innovative institution that offered not only a theological education but also a high school diploma.

Viewed from a strictly sociological perspective, there is no doubt that faith has helped transform and improve millions of lives, not only in the American South but also across Latin America, Asia, Africa and elsewhere.

Education Matters: Dad was the eleventh in a family of fourteen children – but among the first to finish high school. His older brothers and sisters more typically finished fifth grade and then dropped out to work in the cotton mills.

Like faith, education eventually had a transforming effect, providing new opportunities and wider choices to those who had access to it. Several of my Dad's brothers earned their high school equivalency later in life and some went on to college. Again, the power of education is amply demonstrated, both in my father's family and in broader trends around the world.

Demographic Transitions Matter: Even during the Great Depression, a family with fourteen children was unusual. Perhaps more remarkably, each of those children went on to have families – but none went on to have more than three children of their own.

This transition from a very large family living in a rural setting to a small urban-based nuclear family within a single generation is repeated elsewhere in the world. While I grew up with "cousins by the dozens," parents with smaller families are usually able to offer a better economic future for their children. Only one of my nearly fifty first cousins on both my mother and father's side of the family have had more than three children of their own.

Mobility Matters: The extended Addleton family was not especially mobile and most of the second and third generation still live in Middle Georgia. In fact, for very poor families around the world it is often too expensive to move -- in countries that experience extensive out-migration such as Pakistan, Yemen, Tajikistan or the Philippines, it is not typically the poorest of the poor that can finance the departure of a family member to work in the Middle East, Russia or elsewhere; rather it is the slightly more well off that are best positioned to take advantage of these opportunities.

Yet migration, when it is possible, can make a marked difference on income, improving living standards, strengthening educational opportunity and expanding choice. For one of my father's brothers, that opportunity came during World War II when he moved to Delaware to work in a shipyard; for one of my mother's brothers it was the move to Detroit to work in manufacturing when he was demobilized at the end of the war that had the same effect.

I witnessed many of these dynamics as a child but did not really comprehend them at the time. Only much later have I come to understand something of the lives of those that preceded me: "But these were merciful men whose righteousness hath not been forgotten". Only much later have I come to more fully appreciate the legacy they left behind: "The people will tell of their wisdom and the congregation will shew forth their praise".

Having now retired to a house built by my cousin on what was once a pasture on the Addleton farm, Ben Hill Drive is becoming part of my life too. I remember Dad's father – "Papa" – at age seventy, attempting to ride a dirt bike in gathering darkness outside the house where my cousin Bennie now lives. I remember Papa learning to water ski at age seventy-five. I remember asking Papa if Dad ever gave him a "hard time". Papa's reply was immediate and clear: "No, it was me who gave him a hard time!"

Other recollections occasionally spill into my daily life, especially when I walk down Ben Hill Drive and see the cement slab where Dad's mother – "Mama" – milked cows. I also remember the story, related in these pages, of that last meeting with Mama when I was nine years old, a meeting in which I took the final picture of her with a cheap plastic camera, producing a touching black and white photo of her pensive smile.

Always, I am amazed to see that giant wild cedar tree that Dad planted not long after he moved to Ben Hill Drive as a boy, a tree that is now ancient and yet has somehow survived all these years. At the end of the day, all of us are survivors. I love the fact that Dad's youngest brother B.L. lives across the street, that together the two of them now form the "anchor" for those Addletons still living on Ben Hill Drive and in the wider Middle Georgia area.

Thank you, Dad, for the choices you made and the principles to which you dedicated your life. And, as you enter your tenth decade on this wonderful earth, thank you, Dad, for taking the time to write down these fleeting memories, memories that can now be passed on to a new generation of Addletons, making them part of the never-ending chain that connects all of us forever.

Chapter one:
Ben Hill Drive

Our second son Jonathan retired in January 2017 after a 32-year Foreign Service career. He and Fiona now live at 1753 Ben Hill Drive, on the edge of what was once the farm where I grew up. Bettie and I have been living here since our retirement in 1994. We continue to live independently at this address, on the lower level of their home.

The house sits on five acres of what was formerly a 120 acre farm which Papa bought in 1940. Jonathan and Fiona are interested in the history of the property. This is why I am writing these recollections. I write from memory and I hope that readers who discover any mistakes or discrepancies will not hesitate to let me know.

I was born in Macon on November 30, 1929 in what is now the Bloomfield area. The area was rural then. My parents already had ten children, including an infant brother named Claude Robert who died several months before I was born. From short snatches of conversation that I remember from Mama and Papa, they moved the family several times and had lived all over Middle Georgia including in Jones County, Houston County and Bibb County.

Around 1939 or 1940 the Addleton family moved to a 120 acre farm off Clinton Road in Bibb County. Previously, they had lived in an unpainted shack of a house on what is now Graham Road in Jones County, on the other side of Walnut Creek. At the time the road was not paved and had not yet been given a name.

Papa and my older brothers built the Graham Road house from torn-down barn timber. I well remember that house. We had no neighbors living nearby. It was little more than a shack. There was no insulation. Of course, there was also no electricity or running water. I don't know how we survived the cold winters. There were cracks in the walls and cracks in the floors.

Our windows were shutters made from planks. My brother Otha remembers that the older boys would sometimes slip out through the shutters at night. When one of my brothers was returning home through the window, others in the family thought that there was a burglar coming in and attacked him with a bat. He quickly shouted, "Wait, wait, I am your brother".

Papa, Mama and my older siblings farmed the land. My oldest brother John (we called him "Buck") was already married to Frances Hudson so all my other siblings lived in that house including an orphaned first cousin named Felton Johnson whose mother, Ora Lee Gordon, daughter of John Gordon and Anna Marshall, had died at an early age of pulmonary tuberculosis.

My youngest brother B.L. was born in the Graham Road shack in 1933. My sister Louise came home from school after the birth. She said she felt sad for Gloria who was now no longer the "baby" in the family. When I asked where the baby came from, my sister Annie Ruth said that the doctor had brought B.L. in his black bag!

The United States was in the middle of the Great Depression and in those years our shack and the large family living inside of it could have become an iconic photo representing that time, had a newspaper reporter discovered us. However, our basic needs were met.

My sister Velma remembers that our family always had enough to eat, even though it might entail eating the same thing for dinner each evening – fatback, biscuits and syrup. Velma also remembers that B.L. would often be found carrying biscuits in his pocket. On one occasion, she remembers B.L. asking her if there would be biscuits in heaven!

The farm provided our basic food needs. It also helped that the older siblings found jobs. Papa worked as a carpenter for the railroad while some of my brothers and sisters worked several miles away in the Willingham Cotton Mill on Holt Avenue in Macon. They routinely walked to the mill and back until they earned enough money to buy a car.

The Willingham Mill Village and the church that was part of it played an extremely important role in our family. Most of us were baptized in the church and several found their spouses there.

I can recall quite a lot from those early boyhood years on Graham Road. Mostly it was a happy time. It is often said that one's personality is shaped in early childhood so those were critical years for me. The later years spent on the nearby farm situated just off Clinton Road completed my childhood development.

I don't know from whom Papa bought the farm or the price he paid for it. Martha Stine who was and remains our neighbor remembers vaguely hearing that a Mr. Cook sold it to Papa. She also remembers that Mr. Cook had a daughter named Frances and that he owned a lumber yard on Jeffersonville Road. If that is true, he may not have had the time needed to operate a farm.

My guess is that he bought or inherited the land from someone who was a serious farmer. The barn, smoke houses and tenant houses suggest that. Someone reading this recollection might become curious enough to go to the Bibb County Court House and search out the answers.

Our move from Graham Road to Clinton Road was the start of great changes in our family life. The distance was not far – hardly a mile. But it meant that we had moved to a different county, from Jones County to Bibb County.

The house was much better and more attractive than the Graham Road house in which we had previously lived. It faced Clinton Road, also known as US 129. It was named Clinton Road because the next town going north was the historic town of Clinton, Georgia.

Clinton was established in 1808, long before Gray or Macon even existed. When the railway line was built, the tracks were laid a little north of Clinton and a town sprang up along the tracks. This new town was named Gray. Established in 1905, Gray is now a flourishing town and serves as the county seat for Jones County.

Entering Gray, there is a historic marker announcing that once-upon-a-time a town named Clinton had been established nearby. Traces of the town remain. You can walk the historic lanes and see houses in "Old Clinton" dating to the late 1700s.

The house we moved into off Clinton Road was made of white clapboard. I'm not sure but I think that wooden shingles were used to make the hipped roof. The house had a wide front porch with railings and banisters. It had not yet been screened.

Several cement steps led down to a walkway, in turn leading left or right to two gates outside a fence that enclosed a small lawn. The distance from the house to Clinton Road was quite long, leading me to speculate that this small lawn was fenced off to reduce the need for mowing.

The left gate led to a side yard as well as to a dirt driveway coming up the hill from the highway. The right gate provided access to another side yard, this one with a large pecan tree and a brick-lined flower pit for protecting pot plants in winter.

I don't know when our farm house was first built. However, the layout was typical of houses built in the American South during the early 1900s. It had a hallway down the middle and two rooms on each side with one fireplace between each of the two rooms.

Each fireplace had grates to hold the fire; they also included iron covers used to close off the fireplaces during the summer months. On each iron cover was an embossed scene. There was a low metal guard in front of each of the two fireplaces to prevent sparks and ashes from reaching the floor. This was a great change from the large pot-bellied stove in the front room of our drafty Graham Road home.

Our hallway ran from the front porch to a latticed back porch. Our well was located in our backyard, just beyond this latticed porch.

The walls of the rooms and hallway were made of heavy cardboard panels. Brown wooden strips were used to help nail the panels to the wall.

For the first time we had running water and electricity. Each room included a light bulb hanging from the beaded wood ceiling. The windows had large plate glass panes – no more drafty wooden shutters to let the cold wind in! The upper half of the front door was also made of glass and included narrow glass panels on each side.

Some things remained the same when we first moved to our new home. We drew water from a well and had the typical "four rooms and a path" that lead to our outhouse.

This is the house as it was when we moved into it in 1939 or 1940. There would be many changes during the coming years.

Several siblings were included in the move to this new house: Paul, Leon, Louise, Velma, Hilda, Helen, Gloria and B.L. Our orphaned cousin Felton Johnson also remained part of our household. John, Otha, James and Annie Ruth were already married and lived elsewhere.

Although we were now in another county, we continued attending school in Jones County. We simply walked up Clinton Road and boarded the school bus as it turned off Graham Road toward Gray.

My fifth grade teacher during the 1939-1940 school year in Gray was Miss Mae Stewart. I was never tardy but did miss five days of school. I mostly did well though tended to get lower grades in writing and arithmetic. My report card from that year included advertisements from W.C. Abercombie (*"Buy, sale, trade, mules and horses"*), Highland Pharmacy (*"Prescriptions our Specialty"*) and the Bank of Gray.

Someone must have reported that we were living in Bibb County but still going to school in Gray. As a result, sixth grade turned out to my last year in the Jones County school system. We then had to attend school in Bibb County. Luckily, Velma had just graduated from Jones County High School. By that time, only the younger four of us siblings were still in school.

We transferred to Alexander III in Macon and I started seventh grade, taught by Miss Ruth Smith. One of my classmates was named Tommy Olmstead who later became a well-known name in city and county politics.

I spent all of my later boyhood and adolescent years in Bibb County and graduated from Lanier High School in Macon in 1947. That same year I left home to attend Columbia Bible College in Columbia, South Carolina. I did not return to live on Ben Hill Drive again until Bettie and I retired in 1995. Of course, I returned many times for visits over the years, observing the changes that had taken place.

The property off Old Clinton Road where Bibb County borders Jones County is now vastly different. What was once the dirt road leading into the farm is now paved and has access to city services – once referred to as "Ben's Hill," it is now called "Ben Hill Drive," named after my father Ben Addleton.

Some of the changes took place while I still lived on the farm. A kitchen was added to the back of the house and the latticed back porch was enclosed to provide more space. A pump was installed over the well, giving us running water. A corner of the back bedroom was enclosed to build a small bathroom. During my last years living on the farm, I slept on a blue fold-up couch in the hallway.

On December 7, 1946, the Winecoff Hotel in downtown Atlanta burned down and 119 people were killed.

The news must have impressed me deeply. Not long afterwards I went to sleep and dreamed about it. Half awake but still dreaming, I saw a lightning bug flying around the room and heard the click of the fridge turn on. Thinking our house was on fire, I shouted "Fire, Fire"! Imagine my embarrassment when everyone began running out of the house!

Behind our house was the dirt backyard where we played hopscotch and parked the car. The first car I remember was a 1938 Dodge sedan. We also had a one-horse wagon and an old truck on our property.

Across the backyard was a smokehouse where hams were cured. We had hogs in the early years and I vaguely remember Papa butchered them after the first frost. Nearby was a fenced-in vegetable garden.

Beyond the smoke house and the garden was a large barn. It had three rooms and a loft. The middle room was a place for storing corn and farm equipment. There was a machine that shelled corn off the cob. The room on the right was a mule stall and the room on the left was the cow stall. Bales of hay were stored in the loft.

Over the mule stall was an opening where hay was thrown down into a rack for feeding the mules after they returned from plowing. I liked to arrange the bales of hay into tunnels for us kids to crawl through.

In the late afternoon I had to go to the pasture and drive the cows home, herding them through the gate to the lot behind the barn. From there Mama would choose a cow and drive it inside to milk. The ground in the stall became muddy and Papa cemented a small slab where Mama placed her stool for milking. Ironically, the cement rectangle is still there, a momento from the farm where I once lived.

Across the barn and facing the driveway was another small house similar to the smoke house. Mule bridles, ropes, plows and other equipment were kept there.

Continuing up the driveway were two tenant houses for farm helpers. The house on the left was the better of the two. It had four rooms and a front and back porch. The house on the right was made of planks. Later, the house was torn down, revealing a log cabin beneath the planks. People must have been living at this location for a long time.

I remember the occupants of the better house. He was named Mr. Davis and had two daughters, Marie and Catherine. He helped on the farm. Later Uncle Horace and his wife Edith from Arkansas lived there. She smoked a corn cob pipe. Uncle Horace was a top notch auto mechanic.

The other house was occupied by Negroes, as African-Americans were then called. Occasionally other Negroes joined them for a preaching service. One time, hearing the singing, I walked close enough to look inside. There was shouting and one young woman fell on the floor in a trance.

Beyond the tenant houses was the barbed wire fence that enclosed the pasture. The driveway turned right at the house where the Negro family lived and continued into the fields.

I remember little about farming the land. One year Papa planted cotton and my sister Hilda and I picked it one hot summer day. We must have picked several croker (burlap) sacks full because I pretended to collapse on them as if I had a heat stroke. I didn't respond until Hilda panicked!

Later Papa leased what he called some "bottom land" across Clinton Road. I was twelve years old and that was the year I learned to hitch a mule to a plow and plow the land. I plowed round and round the field, breaking up the soil. Then Papa came along and plowed straight furrows for planting.

On one occasion Papa asked me to go home to retrieve a bag of pea seeds. Crossing a dry creek branch on my return, I accidently dropped the bag, spilling some of the seeds on the ground. I covered them with dirt so no one could see them. A few days later, we were walking along the same path and Papa noticed that peas had suddenly sprung up in the dry creek bed. "Who did that"? he asked.

Papa planted okra, tomatoes and watermelon. It was indeed good soil and produced well. We had to harvest it. The okra stung and we wore old socks over our hands to pick it. We rested in the shade of a tree, broke open a watermelon and ate it with our hands. Watermelons and tomatoes have never tasted so good!

Papa and my older brothers loaded hampers of okra and baskets of tomatoes and took them into town to sell. Every time I drive along Gray Highway toward Gray, I remember that I'm driving through a field that we once leased as part of our farm.

We had two neighbors, one on each side of us. Both men were railroad engineers. On our left side were Mr. and Mrs. Stevens. Their grounds were immaculately manicured, right down to the edge of the creek. I never saw Mr. Stevens except when he came into his kitchen at night with the lights on while we were sitting on our front porch.

We did have occasional interaction with Mrs. Stevens, his wife whom we considered "snooty". They had a married daughter who lived in Chicago named Lillian Reynolds. I think her husband went to Northwestern University.

Lillian's son Buck Reynolds was my age and he visited his grandparents in Macon each summer. Mrs. Stevens sent him up to play with me at times and I even spent the night with him once or twice. Mama had to buy pajamas for me to wear. We slept on their screened-in "sleeping porch".

When Mrs. Stevens had her club ladies over for lunch, she always sent Mama a plate of what she served. I only remember potato salad on lettuce.

The Stine family lived on the other side of us. They were the friendly neighbors. Their children were named John, Phillip, Evelyn and Martha. Phillip was a chief petty officer in the Navy and I happened to come to their house when he was home. He was wearing his white uniform and I admired him very much.

According to the 1940 census, the Stine family income in that year was $3,000 – more than six times that of Papa who listed an income of $468 as a loom fixer in the cotton mill; he placed his farm income at zero.

Meanwhile, Paul, age 21 and with a sixth grade education, received an income as $480 as a weaver while Leon, age 18 and with a sixth grade education, received $440 as a twister, also in the cotton mill. Felton, the eighteen-year-old orphan who lived with our family, was a sweeper in the cotton mill but listed no income at all.

Martha Stine and I were the same age and she was a member of the Walnut Creek Gang consisting of me, B.L., Gloria, Helen and Martha. We sometimes sat on Martha's grassy lawn, watching the cars pass by and noting the states and counties mentioned on their license plates.

We had no telephone. However, the Stines gave us permission to give out their phone number to a few people who might need to call us. My brothers Paul and Leon were in the military at the time and they sometimes called us, using our neighbor's telephone number. Someone from the Stine household would holler for us from across the way and one of us would run over to pick up the phone.

Mr. Stine had an orchard which he kept well tended. He showed me how to graft the branch of an apple tree onto another kind of apple tree. He also told me the names of various shrubs and trees around their place.

An unoccupied tenant house was situated near the orchard. The Stine family subscribed to *National Geographic* and stored their old ones there. I would spend hours sitting on the floor reading them with their pictures and stories of foreign places that I could hardly imagine. When I look back at the adults who influenced the direction of my life, the Stine family is numbered among them.

For a short time the Herndon family also became our neighbors. They lived in the nearby gas station belonging to the Stine family. It had long been closed and was now empty, providing them with a place to stay.

Their children were named Rudy, Gail and Twila. Their mother Rose had flaming red hair. They came from somewhere in South Georgia and moved to Macon when their Dad got a job at Robins Air Force Base. Although their stay as our neighbors was brief, they were a fun and memorable family.

The Herndon family later moved to Byron where they lived in a fine house in the center of town. They became prominent residents of Byron and became active members of the First Baptist Church of Byron.

We also knew folks further down the road, both north and south. Further south toward Macon lived Jim Butler who owned a saw mill. I thought of him as a Negro but Martha said he was part Indian. According to the 1940 census, there were actually two brothers – Jim and Eugene, age 64 and age 58 at the time. Their business was called "Excelsior Mill".

Continuing on toward Macon was a long hill that we called "Lowe's Hill," presumably named after the Lowe family who owned a printing shop. Another couple, Gene and Louise

Pickett, lived at the top of the hill. Gene is listed in the 1940 census as an auto mechanic with an annual income of $780.

The Picketts had a daughter named Rose, born in 1939. A small, unused gas station was located beside their house. Both buildings are still standing. The old gas station is now a residence but the house has never been lived in since Gene and Louise died many years ago. Rose wants to keep it as it was.

Next door is a large brick building, also still standing. In my day it was the Crutchfield Gas Station which also sold groceries. This is the point where Upper River Road begins.

Going north across Walnut Creek from our house was Johnson's Gas Station. We walked there to catch the Jones County school bus as it turned from Graham Road into Clinton Road. Of course, that ended when we had to switch to the Bibb County school system and started to use Bibb County school buses instead.

Across the road and in the woods the Johnsons owned and operated a tourist camp. Several cabins were available for overnight check-in. In those days tourist camps were the equivalent of what we now call motels.

Continuing north was a Negro community then referred to as "St. Mark's" which also included St. Mark's Church. Rowena the washerwoman was part of that community and occasionally came to our house to collect dirty clothes to wash for Mama.

(At other times, I would stay home from school on Mondays and help Mama do the wash herself. This involved drawing water from the well and building a fire under the washpot in which the dirty overalls were placed. We also made our own soap, using a mixture of lye and ashes).

Beyond St. Mark's was the Wheeler Nursery. Their son Carl is still living and is a good friend.

Miss Mary and Mr. Samples lived on Graham Road, in Jones County on the other side of Walnut Creek. Mr. Samples operated a dairy farm. Before we moved into the "shack house" on Graham Road, Papa and Mama had lived in a tenant house belonging to Mr. Samples. I think my sister Gloria was born there.

The relationship between Miss Mary and Mr. Samples was always a mystery. I thought of them as husband and wife but later learned that Miss Mary might have been an aunt.

Not long ago Carl Wheeler told me that a woman from Texas had once visited him. She was tracing her ancestry and it led her to Georgia and to Miss Mary who was her ancestor – one of her great great grandmothers. She said that in Texas where she lived, Miss Mary was married and had children. Apparently, a man on a white horse kidnapped her and brought her to Georgia.

Perhaps the kidnapper was Mr. Samples. In any case, their secret went with them to their graves. But they were close family friends. Mama and Papa used to go over to their house and play a card game called Rook. Sometimes Papa and Mama took me with them. I still remember all the pictures on Mr. Samples and Miss Mary's walls.

The major geographic site dominating the area where I grew up was and remains Walnut Creek. We could look across the Stevens' lawn and see it from our front porch.

At times Walnut Creek dried up completely. During heavy rain, it beame a raging river flooding all the way up to the Stevens' house but never flooding the house itself.

Our swimming hole was some distance further up the creek. We reached it by going around the back of the Stevens' property to the "rocks," huge boulders and exposed granite over which the water flows.

These rocks mark the edge of the so-called "Fall Line," where the Appalachian Mountains begin. Cities in Georgia along the Fall Line include Augusta, Macon, Columbus and Milledgeville.

As the water swirls around the rocks, these boulders make parts of the creek deeper than would otherwise be the case. I found one especially deep hole which we often used for swimming. The other kids insisted that I dive into the creek first to scare away any fish and snakes before everyone else jumped in.

I also remember traces of two dams, all that was left of a grist mill that must have been built in previous decades. I could also still see the outline of a canal bed that channeled water onto the wheels that in turn turned the great granite wheels used to grind corn into corn flour.

The Stevens moved at least one of those heavy granite wheels onto their lawn. Mrs. Stevens used it as a lawn table on which to serve her club ladies. Years later, a subsequent owner of the property sold this large granite wheel and with it a piece of history associated forever with our part of Walnut Creek.

Across the creek from our swimming hole and approached from Graham Road was the Blue Bell Lodge. I don't know who owned it. It seems to have been a nightclub and dance hall. It was especially noisy and busy on weekends.

I distinctly remember one night when the music was especially loud and clear. It must have been toward the end of World War II because I still remember some of the lines being bellowed out:

> *There will be a hot time in the town of Berlin*
> *When the Yanks go marching in.*
> *I want to be there boy,*
> *Spreading some joy,*
> *When they take old Berlin.*

That is how I remember this place where I spent so much of my childhood. The area is now totally different from the way I remember it. All the old buildings are now gone.

One of the few traces that remain of the farm where I grew up is the large wild cedar tree that I dug up and planted during the 1940s, when it was just a small sapling pulled up from the nearby woods.

I planted that cedar tree near our house, a structure that has since been torn down. It is now fully grown, providing shade for the nearby brick house, originally built by my older brother Otha and eventually sold, first to the Bush couple and then to Curtis James, an African-American policeman and his wife who still live there.

The cement slab where Mama milked the cows is also still visible, near the James' basketball court. That is all that is left of the farm that I once called home.

Chapter two
Papa and Mama

    I wish I had sat in a rocking chair on the front porch on Ben Hill Drive with Mama and Papa, drawing out from each of them memories of the life they had lived. No doubt most of us have made the same wish. It is now too late for me. Instead, I am writing my own memories of my parents.

    Readers should keep in mind that not all memories are factually correct. Also, interpretations of memories may vary, with different people involved in the same event later recalling different versions of it. Finally, memory itself is fragmented and incomplete, falling short in terms of ever representing the sum total of each life and personality.

    Against that backdrop, the focus here is on my own interactions with my parents as well as my siblings. Their memories, recollections and interactions are undoubtedly different and would almost certainly provide a different perspective.

Papa

May 22, 1888 – October 13, 1982

My father, Benjamin Lark Addleton, was born in 1888, the year that Karl Benz invented the automobile. He was the grandson of a mysterious man, Cyrus Duffey Addleton. Cyrus had come to Georgia from Massachusetts in the 1840s. He married a Macon girl named Eliza Kitchens in 1848. The marriage is recorded in the Bibb County records. She in turn bore him two sons, Robert Edward and Horace Duffey.

I remain puzzled by a notation in the 1850 US census. According to those records, Cyrus and Eliza had an infant son named Mark, born in Cherokee County, Alabama. Soon after, Cyrus disappeared as mysteriously as he had appeared. I don't know what happened to their infant.

Papa's father Robert Edward was one of the Cyrus sons who survived. I have yet to definitively discover Papa's age when his mother passed away. He must have still been a young boy. However, the records indicate that her name was Penny Griffin; some accounts also refer to her as Penny Churchwell Griffin.

Grandpa Robert then married Mary Wilson whom I remember as my step-grandmother. I referred to Mary Wilson Addleton as "Grandma". She died in 1956, when Bettie, David and I were passengers aboard the freighter *Steel King*, making our way across the Atlantic Ocean to Pakistan.

Mama and Papa bore 14 children. All but one of them lived into adulthood. I was their eleventh child. My brother Claude Robert was the tenth and he died of pneumonia before his first birthday. Given that we were so close in age, I wonder how we would have related to each other growing up as brothers. I also wonder how different my growing-up years might have been had he survived.

Much is written about fathers and sons. As for me, I was not close to Papa. I feared him and my fear of him goes back to one incident when I was a very young boy and we were living in the shack on Graham Road.

Mama must have been away for the evening. It was night and Papa and Velma were playing at a card table by the light of an Aladdin kerosene lamp. Helen, Gloria and I were running around the room, chasing each other. I ran into the card table and knocked the lamp to the floor. Papa was furious. In his anger, with his belt or with his leather razor strop, he beat me unmercifully.

When Mama arrived home I was lying on their bed sobbing, with a compulsive catching of the breath. Mama removed my shirt and saw the whelps on my back. She confronted and scolded Papa.

That experience colored my feeling toward Papa all my life. He was short tempered and I made sure never to annoy him. However, as the years passed he made efforts to be a father to his many children, teaching them skills that he thought were necessary in that day and time.

When I was twelve, he taught me how to hitch a mule to a plow, plow a field and drive a wagon. When I was fifteen, he taught me how to drive. Ocasionally he had me give his face a shave.

He also provided fun and entertainment when he could afford it. He took us to the State Fair every year. He was a Mason and took us to the Shriner Circus at the Macon City Auditorium.

He worked as a carpenter at the Central of Georgia Railroad which provided his family with free travel tickets each year. I was very young when we traveled by train to Tybee Island, near Savannah. Years later we traveled together to Wilmington, Delaware to visit my brother Leon who during World War II worked in the shipyards there.

Papa was a heavy drinker and gambler and wasted much of his earnings. Mama knew where he would be on Friday afternoons after he got his pay check. I must have been fifteen then and could drive, so she sent me to a pool hall on Broadway where, half drunk, he was playing pool and drinking. I brought him home.

At age twelve I had been "saved' and baptized at Willingham Baptist Church. Now I was nearing sixteen. I wondered what path my life would take. I asked Papa what classes I should choose during my final years of high school. He replied that I should take business classes in order to get a good job after graduating. Based on his advice, I took bookkeeping rather than Latin.

Meanwhile, my young pastor Y.Z. Gordy challenged me toward missionary service, opening up his study and letting me read books from his personal library by authors such as L.E. Maxwell, H.A. Ironside and D.L. Moody as well as the biographies of a number of well-known missionaries including David Livingston and Adoniram Judson.

At the age of sixteen I set my course toward a life of missionary service abroad. College was a requirement and no one in my family had ever attended college. All my older siblings with the exception of Velma had quit school to go to work and help support the family. I was surely expected to do the same, especially because Papa wasted so much of his earnings.

I put God to the test. I prayed, "Lord if your plan is for me to go to college, change Papa".

Meanwhile, pastor Gordy had already been inviting Papa on hunting trips with him. Papa, now age sixty, must have felt it was time to change since everyone in the family had become church-goers. The friendship had the desired result. Papa answered the altar call, giving his life to Christ and was baptized. He became a different person and his life changed dramatically.

In the fall of 1947 Papa and Pastor Gordy drove me to Columbia, South Carolina where I was enrolled as a freshman at Columbia Bible College, an experience that changed my life. A new world opened up to me, one that introduced me to a broad cross-section of evangelical Christianity. Speakers such as John Stott and Billy Graham spoke in our chapel services, not to mention countless, little-known missionaries from around the world.

Columbia Bible College was a wonderful experience, both inside and outside the classroom. Papa came to my graduation in 1951, an event that included both our senior class hymn (*Lead On, O King Eternal*) and a congregational hymn (*All Hail the Power of Jesus' Name*). Papa also attended my wedding at Mikado Baptist Church in Macon where Bettie and I were married in 1953.

In the summer of 1955 Bettie and I enrolled in a linguistics course at the University of Toronto as part of our preparation for missionary service in Pakistan. My sister Louise drove Mama and Papa to Canada to visit us there. They visited Niagara as part of their trip. It was the first time that Papa set foot outside the United States.

One of our teachers was Dr. Eugene Nida, a noted linguist who developed the dynamic equivalent theory of Bible translation. I introduced Dr. Nida to Papa and they had a brief conversation. As I remember it, Dr. Nida, being a linguist and author of many books about language, was fascinated with Papa's way of talking.

Papa found it difficult to believe that we were leaving for Pakistan and that we would spend more than month on a cargo ship getting there. The last thing he told me when we said our farewells was, "When you set foot on land again, you'll head back home". Our decision to go to Pakistan as missionaries was beyond his imagination.

We received our salary from the Conservative Baptist Missionary Society in Chicago, Illinois each quarter. In the beginning it was not easy to make our meager funds stretch that far before receiving the next payment. Once we came up short and I wrote to Papa for a loan of $200. He sent the full amount immediately.

When Papa reached the age of 89, he worked with his daughter-in-law Mattie to calculate his bank account balance. He then divided the money equally among his living children. We received a check, signed by Papa and dated April 1977, for $636.36. Along with the check was a letter written in Mattie's legible handwriting but dictated by Papa who also signed his name. Papa died five years later at the age of 94.

Mama
November 19, 1894 – June 25, 1966

My mother, Bessie Gordon Addleton, was born in 1894, the year that Coca Cola was first sold in bottles. Her mother was Anna Marshall. Anna had married John Fletcher Gordon. He was a Confederate soldier and is buried in the Dixon Methodist Church cemetery.

The Marshalls and Gordons were among the families that settled in Middle Georgia in the 1800s, along Knoxville Road and Marshall Mill Road, both straddling the county lines of Bibb County and Crawford County near Lizella and Roberta. The cemeteries in this area bear the names of these farming families who lived as part of close-knit communities.

Mama had several sisters and one brother. Unfortunately, I heard little from Mama about her growing up years. Her favorite magazine was *Life*. One of her Marshall uncles owned and operated a grist mill on Eecheconnee Creek near where it crosses Marshall Mill Road. The ruins of Marshall's Mill – or at least parts of the dam that was an essential part of it – still survive.

I'm not sure if Mama grew up on that property. She did speak of living in a house with columns. She also mentioned traveling by train to Byron. She went to a local fair and kept a little vase engraved with her name ("Bessie Gordon") and the date ("1903"). She must have been nine years old at the time.

In retrospect, it is strange that she married outside the Marshall Gordon community to a man whose family name was Addleton. I don't know how Mama and Papa met. Uncle Sam, Papa's half brother, said that Papa took Bessie from plowing a field to marry her; she left the plow and mule in the field to get married!

This fits in well with another story that suggests the two of them had eloped when Mama was sixteen years old. Papa would have been twenty-two years old at the time. Supposedly, she sent a letter to her parents afterwards, informing them of the marriage and asking them to send her clothes and her snuff.

By the time I was born, Mama was raising ten children; there would eventually be three more of us. Mama was also grieving the death of her baby boy Claude Robert, not yet a year old. These were difficult years, I'm sure. Papa often moved the family from place to place, depending on where he could find work. Mama had to set up house over and over again.

My first memories date to when I was three or four. At the time we lived in the shack on Graham Road in Jones County. Mama was in the kitchen and Helen or Gloria and I were playing around her. I picked up a butcher knife and one of my sisters wanted it too. She grabbed the blade. Mama screamed. That scream still stays with me to this day. Fortunately, neither of us was cut.

I also remember Mama sitting in her rocking chair in the living room, drinking a bottle of Coca Cola. I was about three and was kneeling in front of her, begging for a sip. I did this as often as she relaxed with her Coke and she would usually leave a little in the bottom of the bottle for me.

Another memory involves a freshly made cake with coconut frosting. I couldn't resist running my finger aross the frosting to taste it. Mama later discovered what I did and commanded me to fetch a switch from an outside bush. The switching didn't actually hurt that much!

Mama cooked good meals on a wood stove. We had fresh-baked biscuits for breakfast every morning, sopping them with sorghum syrup and slices of fat back. On occasion we might also have grits over which we poured gravy from frying the fat back. Strong black coffee would be percolating on the stove. If we wanted a snack during the day, I would take a leftover biscuit, punch a hole with my finger and pour syrup into it. It was delicious.

Dinner was at noon and typically included black eyed peas, turnip greens, okra and cornbread. I remember digging sweet potatoes out of a mound of straw and dirt, put there in the fall for our table in winter. My favorite dessert was Mama's chocolate pudding over which she spread meringue. For supper we ate leftovers from dinner.

Our Graham Road house had five rooms as well as a front and back porch. Three of the rooms were bedrooms: one for Mama and Papa; one for the boys; and one for the girls.

Each room was furnished with only one or two beds so we must have crowded together at the head and foot of each one. As the little boy going to sleep among several older brothers, I had to sleep at the foot of the bed.

There is an old hillbilly song that captures something of the reality of that time:

They say some folks don't know what it is
Havin' company all over the place
To wrestle for the cover on a winter night
With a big foot sittin' in your face.

Or cold toenails a catchin' your back
And the footboard scrubbin' your head
I'll tell the world you ain't lost a thing
Never sleepin' at the foot of the bed.

I've done it over and over again
In this land of the brave and the free
And in this all fired battle of life
It's left its mark on me.

For I'm always a strugglin' around at the foot
Instead of forgin' ahead
And I don't think it's caused from a doggone thing
But sleepin' at the foot of the bed.

The front room included a big pot-bellied stove to keep us warm in winter. On early winter mornings when it was still dark I would be awakened by Mama calling one of my older brothers to get up and start a fire in the stove. Minutes later, from my bed, I could hear them talking around the table and eating a hurried breakfast. I could smell the fat back frying.

The long table where we ate was made of planks. Long benches were arranged on each side, providing seating for the children. Mama and Papa sat at a straight chair placed at each end of the table.

After breakfast my older brothers left by foot to walk the several miles to work at the Willingham Cotton Mill on Holt Avenue in Macon. Later they bought a car for $35. I was too young to recall the model. However, in later years, after we had moved to the farm off Clinton Road, Papa bought a 1938 Dodge.

Louise drove with Mama sitting beside her. The younger siblings sat in the back seat. She drove that 1938 Dodge to work at the Willingham Cotton Mill every weekday. She also drove us to Willingham Church twice on Sunday and on every Wednesday night. We sometimes commented that our old Dodge knew the way to Holt Avenue and back and didn't even need a driver.

Mama planted flowers – verbena and zinnias especially – in flower beds in our front yard. On warm nights during the summer months she would spread a quilt on the front lawn and we would sleep there throughout the night. I remember waking to look up at the night sky and see what we called "falling stars".

Our youngest sibling B.L. was born in Mama's bedroom on Graham Road. Big sister Annie Ruth kept us in the living room and we were told to keep quiet. A doctor came, driving up in a Model T Ford. He went into the bedroom with a bag in hand. After what seemed like a long time we heard a baby cry. As mentioned earlier, I asked Annie Ruth where the baby came from. She told me that the doctor brought it to our house in his bag!

B.L.'s birth completed our family of fourteen children. Doing the math, it might be said that Mama spent most of her adulthood pregnant, giving birth and raising children. We final four siblings were more like one family, growing up together. Unlike our older siblings, we were able to continue our education through high school. Of the older ten children, only my sister Velma was able to stay in school through twelfth grade.

Our older sisters helped raise us, especially Louise. Louise prepared me for school each morning, making sure my hair was combed and my ears, neck, hands and feet were clean. We went barefoot to school in Jones County. I don't remember how often we bathed all over – probably it was once a week in a tin tub. Mama with help from Louise made sure that I was clean when I first boarded the Jones County school bus at the age of five.

School was eleven miles away and I still remember the route. At the time only Clinton Road was paved. All other roads on the route to Gray were dirt and on rainy mornings the bus sometimes slid into a muddy ditch.

A little girl with dark brown hair and dark eyes rode the same school bus with us. Her name was Bettie Simmons, my sister Helen's friend. Her brother James was my buddy and her sister Sarah was my sister Hilda's friend. They lived on a dairy farm down the road from us. I ignored her in those years. Many years later Bettie became my wife.

Everything changed when we moved across the county line to Bibb County. For a year we had surreptitiously continued in the Jones County school system by simply walking up the road and boarding the Jones County school bus.

Once this was discovered and we enrolled in the Bibb County school system, we boarded the school bus in front of our house. All four of us entered grammar school together at Alexander III only a couple miles away.

I remember being embarrassed walking into my seventh grade classroom that first morning, barefoot and in short pants as we did in Jones County. Now we were in a city school, surrounded by city children. All the other boys wore shoes and long pants. Mama understood and the next day I wore my church clothes – long pants and shoes.

Alexander III was located in one of Macon's most affluent neighborhoods. The Jones County School must have given me a good education because I fitted in well scholastically into this new one.

I graduated from grammar school at the end of that year and Mama proudly attended the occasion. Mama was always there for special occasions. In terms of education, she had graduated from fourth grade. As for Papa, he is listed in the 1940 census as having had a second grade education.

ROTC was compulsory at Sidney Lanier High School for Boys, named after the locally famous nineteenth century Macon poet Sidney Lanier (our school football team at the time was known as "The Poets"). Occasionally on a Wednesday we would march in dress parade. I was proud to see Mama standing with the other parents watching as we passed by.

As a high schooler, I sang in the Glee Club. We gave a concert at the end of the school year at the old Wesleyan College Auditorium on College Street. Once again, Mama was there too. I remember two of the songs that we performed: *Dona Nobis Pacem* and *Stout Hearted Men*.

Mama's life was hard. She bore fourteen children between 1912 and 1933 in the rural Deep South, raising most of them at a time when the Great Depression was in full swing. She herself was born as part of a post Civil War generation, raised during a time when the effects of that war were still being played out.

I have often wondered how she survived. Underneath the surface, she was a woman of impressive intelligence, character and beauty. At special events she wore hats and gloves. Her hair was pulled back in a bun. Occasionally I watched as she loosened the bun, bending over and brushing her long flowing hair. Much later she had her hair cut because the pain from a torn rotator cuff prevented her from lifting her arms to pull it back.

Papa and Mama celebrated their fiftieth wedding anniversary in April 1961, receiving a write-up in the *Macon Telegraph*, the same local newspaper that a few years earlier had run another article about them under the headline "Addletons Say Big Family Easy to Raise as Small". That article had quoted Mama and Papa as saying, "A large family is no more trouble than a small one, once you get used to it".

Approximately one hundred friends and relatives attended Mama and Papa's Golden anniversary celebration on Ben Hill

Drive, arranged by my sister Louise in her home where Mama and Papa also lived. Among other things, the *Macon Telegraph* noted that Mama and Papa had 24 grandchildren.

Bettie and I were home on leave from Pakistan four years later, during 1965-1966. At the age of 72, Mama was now dying from congestive heart failure. Several times she rallied when she seemed near death. Somehow she kept holding on to life.

We had tickets to sail on a ship back to Pakistan. However, we cancelled our travel plans while waiting for her imminent death. She knew that we were scheduled to depart and she told us that we belonged in Pakistan, that we should not stay in Macon any longer.

This time we booked our return by air and the day came for us to leave. B.L. was waiting to take us to the airport while we said our goodbyes. David, Jonathan and Nancy came into Mama's room to say their final goodbyes in turn. I suppressed my emotions while I held her hand and prayed.

As we were leaving her bed, Jonathan snapped a picture of her lying there. It was a cheap plastic camera with a roll of black and white film inside. When we were exiting the airplane at Rawalpindi Airport a couple of days later, he dropped the camera on the tarmac and it fell open. He quickly retrieved the camera and closed it and we continued on our way to Murree.

Jonathan was curious to to see if the photos would be any good, given that the camera had opened and the film had been exposed to light. When the developed pictures were returned from the film shop in Murree, to his and our surprise a few pictures including the photo of Mama survived!

Mama was half sitting up in bed, watching us leave the room. She did not appear sad; in fact, she had a faint smile. It was the last photo of her before her death three weeks later. I had copies made for each of my siblings. Of course, we treasure it.

On June 25, 1966, a telegram arrived from Velma to inform us that Mama had died. I was away with Jonathan at

Bach Hospital sixty miles over the mountains near Abbottabad where Jonathan's appendix was being removed. Bettie phoned to tell me.

I took the news as just a matter of fact until I was traveling by train down to Sind, leaving the family in Murree for the summer school session. Alone on the train, the finality of Mama's death struck me and I cried for a bit.

Four years later when we returned to Macon for furlough Velma's husband William took me to Mama's grave. I laid a long stem red rose on it and prayed a prayer of thanks for Mama's life.

Chapter Three
Brothers and Sisters

Ben and Bessie Addleton had fourteen children, giving me thirteen brothers and sisters. Twelve of those siblings survived into adulthood. Memories of my siblings follow below, thoughts that emerge at random and in no particular chronological order.

My main motivation in recalling these memories and writing them down is the thought that my grandchildren – and perhaps some of my many nieces and nephews – might at some point be interested in this family history, a history in which many of the precious people that enriched my life have by now passed away. Indeed, only three of Ben and Bessie's fourteen children still survive: my sister Helen, my brother B.L. and myself, all of us in our eighties.

John Forest Addleton
February 19, 1912 – March 10, 1974

My oldest brother John was already seventeen years old when I was born and World War I had not yet started when he came into the world. The family called him "Buck" – until our sister Hilda married Buck Mixon; then everyone had to revert to calling John by his real name.

I only really knew John when he was already an adult. In fact, all my older brothers were more like uncles to me, given the difference in our ages. I also didn't know John apart from his wife, both having married when I was still a toddler. Her name was Frances Hudson. Everyone loved her. Perhaps her family and the Addleton family were neighbors during the years when the Addletons lived in Jones County.

John and Frances had one son whom we called Johnny. He and his uncle (my brother) B.L. were nearly the same age. Johnny passed away in a hospital in Milledgeville in Baldwin County in 2017 after a long illness.

John worked on small planes at Herbert Smart Airport in Macon and he arranged for me to work there one summer. I learned to crank a plane by pulling down the propeller for the pilot and then jumping out of the way when the engine started. Once I accidentally discharged a fire extinguisher at a hangar where I was working and the foam spread everywhere!

John and my brother Paul later worked at Red Dog Airport near Cochran, maintaining small crop dusters. When Robins Air Force Base opened, John started to work there, turning that job into a life-long career.

Many years later John and Frances divorced. He then married Bessie Rogers whom I did not know because I was in Pakistan. John and Bessie had a daughter named Darlene who is very much a part of the Addleton family. We also welcomed her husband Robert Rozier into the family when they married. They have a daughter named Lindsey.

In March 1974 B.L. sent a telegraph that reached us in Hyderabad, the town in southern Pakistan where we lived at that time: "John passed away at 7:30 Sunday night".

Bennie Otha
October 6, 1913 – July 17, 2005

Otha was five years old when World War I ended. Somewhere I saw a picture of John and Otha as children, both dressed in little army uniforms. As with John, Otha seemed more like an uncle than a brother to me during my own growing up years.

My first memory of Otha is when he married Mattie Stevens. They lived in the Willingham Mill Village on Holt Avenue. Lanier High School which I attended was just up the hill. I used to walk down to see them and sometimes I spent the night with them in their home.

Otha and Mattie were both active in Willingham Baptist Church. As a result of their influence, the rest of the Addleton family were baptized and joined the church.

Otha and Mattie had one child, Diane. She was beautiful, both as an adult and as a child. In fact, Bettie and I asked her to be flower girl at our wedding. We had started dating one summer when I was home from seminary in New Orleans. At the time our family car was a big black Packard that looked more like a hearse. When I arrived at Bettie's house for a date, her sisters announced loudly, "Bettie, the hearse is here"! She was a lot happier when I showed up in Otha's small new yellow Studebaker.

When Willingham Cotton Mill closed and the mill village disappeared, Otha and Mattie lived in various places, starting with our family home on Ben Hill Drive. When Papa sold the farm, Otha claimed some nearby acreage and built a lovely red brick house where our old family home once stood. In fact, the cedar tree that I planted nearby as a boy is still there, an ancient tree by now, more than 75 years old.

Otha worked numerous jobs. One was running a truck stop on Gray Highway. As I remember it, my sister Gloria's husband Dude bought it or built it and then asked Otha and Mattie to operate it with them.

Otha was not educated in a formal sense. However, he often taught Sunday School or preached in various Middle Georgia churches. He was not a brilliant public speaker but he was very humble and sincere and would sometimes shed tears when teaching, preaching or praying. His audiences loved him.

Later he sold insurance for a large insurance company. Going from house to house to sell policies and collect monthly payments, he often sold more than the other agents. The company rewarded him and Mattie with trips to Hawaii and Spain which they loved.

As I mentioned, Otha and Mattie had a beautiful daughter named Diane who was flower girl in our wedding. She later married but tragically died with her young husband in a car accident on the road to Atlanta before the Interstate was built. This would have been in 1965 or 1966 and we happened to be in the United States at the time, visiting a supporting church in Iowa. We drove through the night and reached Macon in time to attend her funeral, one of the saddest events in Addleton family history.

Mattie's grief over Diane's death continued for many years. All of us were very saddened by what had happened. Otha and Mattie lived long and full lives. The two of them are now buried next to Diane in Evergreen Cemetery off Houston Avenue in Macon.

James Edward Addleton
November 9, 1915 – April 1983

James was another brother who as a child seemed more like an uncle to me. Mama said that when he was growing up he occasionally had seizures. She put a spoon in his mouth to prevent him from biting his tongue.

I must have been about four when he began dating Lillian Black, daughter of Chester and Pearl Black who lived near Willingham Mill Village. We were living on Graham Road at the time and he brought her to our house which was more like a shack, without electricity, running water or an inside toilet.

James and Lillian arrived in a small car; Otha and Mattie might have been with them. Perhaps they were returning from church because they were dressed well. Mattie and Lillian or perhaps both of them ran to the outside toilet in the rain. They were wearing the kind of dresses that shrink when wet and they were very worried. It is strange that a memory like this should surface after all these years.

James was an expert brick layer and laid bricks during the construction of the Bankers Life Insurance building in Macon, now the home of city government offices. He and Lillian lived on Lawton Avenue, next door to her parents. They had two children, Ted and Jerry.

James became very active in the nearby Willingham Baptist Church. He was the first person who asked me about "loving Jesus". At the time I was about four years old.

Years later he began to feel that God was calling him into ministry. He moved his family to Newton, Mississippi to enroll in Clarke College there. This college accepted students who felt called to preach but had not graduated from high school, offering them both a high school diploma and an associate college degree.

I visited James and Lillian there. I was impressed with Lillian and how well she seemed to cope with this new kind of life. Their income was low and Lillian learned to cut corners to make ends meet. Seeing a jar filled with soap pieces, I assumed that she used them to wash clothes.

While I was visiting, Lillian decided to have chicken for dinner. James was at college. She bought a live chicken and went to the backyard to kill it. We planned to wring its neck, just as our parents used to do.

I volunteered to do the needful, having watched Mama do it in years past. I tried a couple of times but it didn't die. Then Lillian tried ferociously, throwing it violently on the ground to watch it die. But the stubborn chicken got up and ran away and still didn't die. I can't remember if we actually had fried chicken that night. Perhaps James came home and slaughtered it.

James went on to Mississippi College near Jackson, later serving as a pastor in Mississippi. During that time they divorced and Lillian married a chiropractor. Lillian had a daughter in Greenville, Mississippi where she lived for the rest of her life.

As for James, he returned to Macon and served as pastor of Ruth Baptist Church in Bleckley County. He later married someone named Flo who was a nurse. They had one daughter named Pam. James died of throat cancer in Florida in April 1983 and I conducted his funeral there.

Annie Ruth Addleton Cranford
November 29, 1918 – September 24, 1996

Annie Ruth was my oldest sister. She married Cecil Cranford in 1935 when I was only five years old. We called her husband "Buddy".

Interestingly, there is another Annie Ruth Addleton – a cousin who was part of what we called the "Rocky Creek Road" Addletons, to distinguish them from those who lived on Ben Hill Drive.

My first memory of our Annie Ruth was when we lived on Graham Road and she and Buddy lived across Walnut Creek in an old house with John and Frances. We had to cross the creek on a log to get there. At night we carried a lighted torch to see. Once I spent the night and Buddy had me bring in wood for the stove.

Of course, both those houses disappeared long ago. Our Graham Road house was torn down when a new subdivision was built. The remains of the house across the creek survived as a pile of lumber for a long time before that too disappeared.

Annie Ruth was in our Graham Road house when my youngest brother B.L. was born. She kept me and my two younger siblings out of the room while the doctor delivered our baby brother. Annie Ruth later had two children, Eric and Ellen.

Although Annie Ruth was much older than I, we became very close and enjoyed being together. She seemed proud of me and I appreciated her interest and attention. Tape recorders had not yet been invented but she had a device that could cut records and asked me to record my testimony.

Andrew Paul Addleton
September 10, 1919 – August 3, 2009

I was ten and living in the Clinton Road house and I remember sleeping in the same room with Paul and Leon. I was trying to sleep and they were talking about girls. It must have been about their girlfriends whom they were going to marry. These were the first siblings that seemed more like brothers rather than uncles to me.

The family was changing. I can barely remember a time when we hosted occasional barn dances in the Graham Road house. In those days my older siblings also drank alcohol and smoked cigarettes.

Otha and Mattie were living in the Willingham Mill Village and Willingham Baptist Church was reaching out to the "unsaved". Young adults were having Saturday night prayer meetings, going from home to home in the village as a witness to their faith. They sang songs, gave testimonies about their conversion experiences and talked about the trials of living a Christian life. Usually the young women wept as they talked.

I remember one song especially well:

> *I feel like travelin' on,*
> *I feel like travelin' on,*
> *My heavenly home is bright and fair,*
> *I feel like travelin' on.*
>
> *The devil wears a hypocrite shoe,*
> *I feel like travelin' on;*
> *If you don't watch out,*
> *He'll slip it on you,*
> *I feel like travelin' on.*

The time came for Otha and Mattie to have a prayer meeting in their house. They served fried chicken and invited Paul and Leon, both of whom arrived with a half pint in their overalls. They hid the whiskey in the shrubbery before going inside.

Both Paul and Leon were converted that night, leaving their whiskey in the shrubbery where they had hidden it. Our life style changed dramatically. Sins shunned in those days included picture shows (movies), drinking, mixed bathing, dancing, card playing and so on. Preachers condemned such behavior.

Mama stopped using her snuff and other family members stopped drinking, smoking and barn dancing. Smoking was perhaps the hardest habit to quit. After one sermon, Paul and Leon asked the preacher to pray for them to leave it behind.

Mama invited the preacher to have Sunday dinner with us. After eating, they all went out to the hog pen. They threw their packet of cigarettes to the hogs and the hogs immediately devoured them. That was the end of their smoking habit.

Paul married Mary Davis, a girl living outside the mill village. She and her family were Pentecostal and part of a touring group that travelled all over the Southeast. Her brother played the guitar and Mary sang and played the piano by ear. When she married Paul, she quit the traveling music group though she and her family remained close.

During World War II Paul joined the Army Air Force, as it was then called. After training he was posted in North Africa and was part of a crew that maintained the planes that were pushing the enemy through Mussolini's Italy and toward Hitler's Nazi Germany.

Paul was not granted leave and was unable to return home for several years. This was very difficult for Mary. When he finally was given leave, I saw him for the first time in his uniform on Otha and Mattie's front porch. Paul and Mary had one child, Paulette.

Mary suffered a nervous breakdown in the late forties, almost certainly attributable to the years that she had been separated from Paul when he had been away fighting in the war. Of course, this was also extremely traumatic for Paul.

She recovered well and Paul continued his career in aviation. He worked for a time at Moody Air Force Base near Valdosta, Georgia. Later he worked at Robins Air Force Base until he retired. At one time he also pastored a Pentecostal church in Macon.

Later in life Paul and Mary lived in the Bloomfield area of Macon. Eventually, they entered a nursing home. Paul passed away first and Mary lingered for quite a long time afterward.

Mary suffered from dementia during the closing months of her life and did not recognize me during my occasional visits. But she seemed to be mouthing the words of hymns and tapping her fingers as if playing the piano, perhaps recalling her early years as a member of a traveling gospel singing team. I was asked to conduct her funeral.

William Leon Addleton
August 10, 1921 – January 1996

Paul and Leon were born two years apart and lived similar lives until they married. Leon too had a conversion experience in the Willingham Mill Village, similar to what Paul had experienced.

Leon went on to marry Hilda Glass who had grown up in the mill village. She was one of five or six girls born to Raymond and Leila Glass. Their house attracted lots of young people.

World War II was raging and it seemed that Leon would soon be drafted. To delay that possibility, Leon moved Hilda and little Larry to Wilmington, Delaware. There he worked in the shipyards.

Papa was working at Central of Georgia Railroad and was given tickets that allowed Papa, Mama, Hilda's sister Eloise and me to visit. Troops were filling the train cars and some of them were sleeping in the aisles. This was in 1943, during the middle of the war.

We changed trains in Washington, DC. While waiting for our connection to Wilmington, we sat in one of the huge benches in Union Station and ate the fried chicken that Mama had brought with her. I looked out the train window and saw the dome of the U.S. Capitol.

Once in Wilmington, Eloise and I went to a movie that must have been within walking distance of the house where we were staying. Lucille Ball was the star in *Best Foot Forward*. It may have been one of her first major films. I think she played the role of a cheerleader at a college football game. The song she sang was called *Buckle Down Winsocki*.

Papa and Leon traveled to Philadelphia on one day so we must have stayed in Wilmington for several days. Not long afterwards Leon was drafted into the army. Hilda came to live with us and it was very difficult for her to be separated from Leon. She stayed in the bedroom crying for much of the time.

After basic training Leon was sent by ship, along with hundreds of others, to the Pacific. Before the ship reached its destination, Japan had surrendered and the war was over. Leon's ship then returned to the United States and he was released from his military service.

Leon returned to Macon and started working at the Macon Linen Company. Their daughter Marveen was born during this time. Leon seemed restless working at secular jobs. He felt that God was calling him to preach. In preparation for ministry, he took his little family to Mississippi where he enrolled in Clark College, the same school that James had also attended.

After two years Leon and his family returned to Macon where he continued his studies at Mercer University, receiving a Bachelor's degree. The family lived in campus housing and Leon was called to be pastor at Willingham Baptist Church where the Addleton family had such deep connections.

After serving at Willingham, Leon accepted a call to Third Street Baptist Church on Third Street in Macon. People at both Willingham and Third Street Baptist loved Leon and Hilda. They could have stayed in Macon for the rest of their lives and enjoyed a very fruitful ministry.

However, Leon felt the need to go to seminary. So the four of them – Leon, Hilda, Larry and Marveen – moved to Wake Forest, North Carolina, near Raleigh and Leon enrolled in Southeastern Baptist Theological Seminary.

After some years in North Carolina, Leon and Hilda must have had a yearning to return to Georgia. Northside Baptist Church in Warner Robins called Leon to be their pastor. Leon and Hilda bought a house in Warner Robins and spent nineteen happy years serving the people at Northside Baptist Church. It was a sad day for Northside when they retired from the ministry.

Leon took a couple of interim pastorates including Houston Lake Baptist and Antioch Baptist in Taylor County. Then Leon's health began to decline and he left the ministry altogether. By that time, Bettie and I had retired from our years of service in Pakistan and Leon recommended me to become Antioch's pastor. I served there for fourteen years, retiring from that ministry in 2010 at the age of eighty. People at Antioch Baptist Church spoke lovingly of Leon and Hilda and their ministry.

In light of Leon's declining health, Larry and Marveen wanted their parents to live close by. They moved to Raleigh, North Carolina where Leon passed away. His memorial service was held at Northside Baptist Church in Warner Robins.

Louise Addleton Duffey
June 28, 1923 – November 29, 2010

As far as I know, my sister Louise was given no middle name. She assisted Mama in taking care of me, dressing me and combing my hair before I headed off to school in Jones County. Although as smart as others in the family, she dropped out of school earlier than her other sisters except for perhaps Annie Ruth.

Louise also married later in life than the rest of us. She became the anchor of the family, taking on the responsibility of caring for Mama and Papa in their old age.

When she married Henry Duffey, she remained in Mama and Papa's house until our parents passed away. It was right that Louise and Henry should inherit the house and it is appropriate that their youngest son Bennie continues to live there to this day. Louise and Henry's other son Tim became a pastor, ministering in churches in the Florida panhandle.

Henry died in the Dublin Veterans Home while Louise died in the Eastside Nursing Home. Henry was active in the Gideon movement distributing Bibles. He also regularly led services in the Macon jail on Sunday afternoons.

Our children remember Louise as a loving, nurturing mother. On occasion they stayed with the family on Ben Hill Drive overnight when Bettie and I visited churches during furloughs from our work in Pakistan. They also remember Louise as an excellent cook, preparing wonderful breakfasts.

Velma Addleton Whitehead
November 12, 1924 — September 7, 2004

Velma was the first in our family to finish high school, graduating from high school in Jones County. She had a legible cursive handwriting. Not long after completing high school, she married William Whitehead who had served in the Navy. They had three daughters, Carol, Jeanette and Gena.

Velma and William built a house on the dirt road that became Ben Hill Drive, spending the rest of their life there. Their daughter Carol later built a house nearby, as did Gena and her husband Jim Wood. Several years later our second son Jonathan bought Jim's and Gena's house which is where Bettie and I now live in retirement.

Velma was my sibling who wrote us regularly during all the years that we lived and worked in Pakistan. She sent us photos of family events regularly. She also faithfully packaged and sent the Sunday edition of the Macon Telegraph to us in Pakistan each week. In that way, we were able to keep up with happenings in both our family and in Middle Georgia.

Both Velma and William died in Macon. Their daughter Gena carries on the tradition of hosting an Addleton Christmas party on the Saturday before Christmas each year. That annual family tradition to which all members of the extended Addleton clan are invited has continued for more than seventy years.

Hilda Nevada Addleton Mixon
September 18, 1926 — October 28, 2014

I was close to Hilda in age — she was just three years older than I. I don't know how she got her middle name though there must be an intriguing story behind it.

I have the impression that Hilda didn't much like school. In any case, she dropped out at around seventh grade. I do know that she was good at arithmetic and could do long division. When I became sick in fourth grade (when long division was taught) and couldn't attend school for several months, she taught me how to do it and I passed the teacher's test on that subject.

Hilda worked several jobs in Macon. One was as an elevator operator in the Banker's Insurance Building, viewed at the time as Macon's first "high rise" building. She met several lifelong friends there. She married Buck Mixon and they had two children, Ricky and Renee.

Hilda was an understanding and sympathetic person. When anyone in the family seemed to be misunderstood, she stood on their side. She was a comforting person as well. When I suffered a brain hemorrhage in retirement, I went into deep depression. As I recuperated, she phoned me every day, helping to lift me out of it.

Hilda and Buck lived on Lake Sinclair in their later years. Buck died tragically in a car accident near Milledgeville. Hilda remained a widow for quite a few years before she also passed away.

Claude Robert Addleton
May 30, 1928 — February 12, 1929

Claude Robert, the sibling nearest to me in age, died before reaching his first birthday. He is buried in the old Shiloh Primitive Baptist Church Cemetery on Columbus Road in Macon.

Hubert Franklin Addleton
November 30, 1929 —

I was born ten months after my brother Claude Robert died. As of this writing, there are now only three of us left. I am the oldest and will probably pass away before my sister Helen and my brother B.L., the youngest in the family.

Helen Virginia Addleton Tucker
March 27, 1931 —

My only surviving sister Helen still lives in Macon with her husband James who was drafted into the Army during the Korean War. Later he joined the Air National Guard, serving for more than twenty years and regularly attending the National Guard conventions after completing his service.

Both Helen and James were nineteen when they married. He later graduated from Georgia College in Milledgeville. He also worked at Robins Air Force Base for many years, eventually retiring at the age of eighty.

Helen and James have had many opportunities to travel, visiting every American state. They both sang in the choir at Ingleside Baptist Church. Helen also was a volunteer for many years, serving in the Medical Center Auxiliary where she helped and encouraged patients during their hospital stay.

Helen and James have three children, Mike, Judy and Janet. They also have several grandchildren. We see Helen and other members of her family from time to time and appreciate our many interactions.

Each year Helen supports the St. Jude's Hospital fundraising campaign by buying raffle tickets. Remarkably, in 2018 her number was drawn and she won a brand new custom built home in Warner Robins.

At this point in her life she was not willing to move, despite having been given a beautiful new house – so the house was sold and Helen and James have benefitted from the proceeds of it. The extended family also benefitted and the following Christmas Helen and James took their entire family including children and grandchildren on a memorable week-long visit to Disney World in Florida!

Gloria Mae Addleton Haskins
September 9, 1932 – October 25, 1975

My youngest sister Gloria was called "Glory Mae" when we were growing up. Somewhat taller than average, she had brown hair and eyes and was very pretty.

We were the final four of fourteen siblings. I think she was born on the Sample place, further up Graham Road. Although born at the beginning of the Great Depression, life would later get a little better for all of us.

We started school in Jones County. However, when we moved to Bibb County we eventually had to transfer to the Bibb County school system. We attended Alexander III in the Baconsfield area. After that, the girls attended Lanier Junior High School for Girls and Miller Senior High School for Girls.

At that time segregation was still very much in place, based on both race and gender. Our education in Bibb County was very good, as evidenced by Gloria's expertise in running the Truck Stop and other businesses with her husband Dude in later years.

We had a lot of fun growing up on the farm on Clinton Road. I can't remember specifically everything we did but we played, swam in the creek and enjoyed the annual State Fair. I remember the two of us as "leaders" of the Walnut Creek Gang which we helped form – the other two members included Martha Stine and my brother B.L. We loved our childhood.

The pecan tree that we climbed as members of the Walnut Creek Gang still stands.

After high school Gloria worked in the Willingham Cotton Mill where she met and married Dude Haskins, also a mill worker. They lived in Willingham Mill Village. We were in Pakistan at the time and the news shocked and disappointed me because I was hoping that both Gloria and Helen would go to college.

It turned out to be a good marriage. Dude, although not educated in a formal sense, was very intelligent with a good sense for business. They soon left the mill and built and operated several businesses. Very late in life, while in his eighties, Dude finally learned to read and write.

One of the first businesses that Gloria and Dude opened was a Truck Stop on Gray Highway which included a restaurant. Writing to me in Pakistan, she recalled the early days of integration and the first African-American family to come into the Truck Stop restaurant to eat. "I returned to my room and cried," she related to me. "Then I returned to serve the African American family and never looked back".

Gloria and Dude designed and built a lovely brick home in the woods behind their Truck Stop. We lived in another of their houses on Joycliff Road during our first furlough back in the United States during 1960-1961. They built other businesses over the years as well and were understandably proud of each of them.

Gloria and Dude had two boys, Andy and Lark. And then melanoma cancer sadly appeared on Gloria's leg. At first her treatment seemed to work. But then the cancer returned and spread. Gloria went through various treatments.

During those years we were in Pakistan and Gloria corresponded with us often. Acknowledging that her cancer was terminal, one letter asked us to pray that she might live long enough to see her two boys grow up. She is buried next to Mama and Papa.

Bob Lawrence Addleton
November 6, 1933 –

Stories about my youngest brother B.L. have appeared throughout this narrative. Once during his growing up years he disappeared and everyone searched for him. Some feared that he might have wandered down to Walnut Creek and perhaps even drowned there. But after all the anxiety, he was eventually found sleeping soundly underneath his bed.

B.L. later joined the Navy, doing a stint on a tanker called the *Marias* that fueled aircraft carriers and other ships in the Mediterranean. After completing his military service, he spent his career working at Robins Air Force Base.

He and his wife Betty Anne have two children, Chris and Robin. Chris attended Georgia Tech and Robin attended the University of Georgia, making the annual football game between the two rival schools especially interesting. Robin and our daughter Nancy share the same birthday -- Nancy was born on July 5, 1959 and Robin was born exactly one year later.

We were in Pakistan when B.L. returned to Macon and married Betty Anne who was also from Macon in February 1958. Their first house was the old tenant house on Ben Hill Drive. Later they built a beautiful new ranch-style house at the top of the hill. Betty Anne's father and mother – Mr. and Mrs. Law – then moved into the old tenant house. When they passed away, the tenant house was torn down and B.L. used the timber to build a shed.

B.L. and Betty Anne were always very hospitable to our two boys when they returned to the United States to go to college. On occasion David and Jonathan would stay with them for days at a time.

Jonathan also spent most of one summer with B.L. and Betty Anne when he and their son Chris worked as laborers on a bush crew at the Rural Electrification Administration (REA) in Gray. Jonathan would come home with ticks. On one occasion, Betty Anne even had to help him remove a tick from his ear. In addition, B.L. and Betty Anne very kindly allowed us to store our personal items in their basement all those years when we were living and working in Pakistan.

Now B.L. and I are growing old together on Ben Hill Drive, the place where both of us spent so much of our childhoods. He lives across the road from us. We see each other often, the last of the boys in a large family that was once full of them.

Chapter Four
Calling

How did it happen that I became a missionary, living and working in an Islamic country on the other side of the world for 34 years? To answer that question, I have to follow a line of events in my family that led me, Bettie and little David to board a cargo ship in New York and start the five-week journey to Pakistan. There my life would be totally different from that of the Addleton family in which I was born and raised.

Life was a struggle for families in the rural South when I was born. The men worked hard in the fields. Saturday nights were for fun and drinking. Sundays were for playing baseball. In the shadowy memory of my very early years there were occasional dances held on the sawdust floor of our barn on Graham Road. There was live music, dancing and alcohol. Church-going was not part of the picture. This would soon change for my family.

Textile mills had moved to the South from New England. Several were built in Macon during the early 1900s. The owners built what were called "mill villages" to house the workers and their families. Poor tenant farmers left the fields for the factory. They raised their families in the village next to the mill. Although salaries were low, life was easier and more secure than working in the fields and having to worry about the vagaries of weather.

The Addleton family is also part of this history. A couple of years ago Billie Coleman published a book of photographs titled *Central Georgia Textile Mills* (Arcadia Publishing, 2017), documenting in pictures this aspect of Macon history.

"People from all over the rural areas of Central Georgia flocked to the mills for a chance at a steady, decent income and possible amenities," she writes. "Workers were lured to textile mills by the opportunity for the whole family to work in the mills and have housing provided . . . In the early 1900s, the labor force of the mills consisted of men, women and children. Children as young as five years were working at the mills for hours a day. Sometimes even younger children were used as lunch carriers or helpers".

Broadus Willingham built a cotton mill on Holt Avenue, a block off Vineville Avenue. He lived in a mansion several blocks away and was an active member of Vineville Baptist Church. He initiated the starting of a mission church in the mill village for the workers and their families and built an attractive white clapboard church with a bell tower and a steeple that still stands. It was named Willingham Baptist Church and its congregation and pastors later set me on the path to become a foreign missionary. I doubt if the "mother church" on Vineville ever influenced its own members as greatly!

The Willingham Mill Village drew many families off the farms and into what became a close-knit, caring community. Papa's two older brothers raised their large families there. One relative even lost an arm in a carding machine, an incident that eventually was taken to court and is described in the legal records of Bibb County.

Papa also worked in the mill, at least for a short time; in the 1940 census, he is listed as a loom fixer with an annual income of $468 dollars for that year. Ten years earlier, in the

1930 census, he is shown as living on Second Street in Macon in a home valued at $3,000.

Papa must have moved from that Second Street address in Bibb County to the Graham Road address in Jones County. He must have also continued his work as a carpenter for the Central of Georgia Railroad company, knocking down box cars. Some of the wood that he retrieved from that job was used to build Mama's dream house on what was first a farm and many years later became Ben Hill Drive.

My older brothers got jobs in the mill. They walked from Graham Road in Jones County to the mill on Holt Avenue, a distance of about five miles. Later they earned enough money to buy a car.

Most of my siblings worked in the mill. Several married into mill families and lived in the village. Otha married the daughter of one of the mill foremen and moved into the village. Tom Collins, acting minister of the church and a highly respected layman, married them.

Mama and my siblings began to attend church "every time the doors opened". By then Louise was the oldest of my siblings still at home. She worked in the mill and drove us to church and back in our 1938 Dodge.

Each spring and fall Willingham Baptist Church held a week of meetings called "Revival". An evangelist or pastor from another church was invited to preach. One notable preacher was a young Mercer ministerial student named Clinton Sheehan. He married the daughter of another mill foreman. At the end of the sermon, an "Invitation" hymn was sung and often several walked down the aisle to accept Christ as their Savior and join the church.

The song "*Just As I Am*" was sung most often and regularly repeated over and over while the evangelist spoke to those who responded to the invitation. Another song that I still remember went as follows:

"Almost persuaded," now to believe;
"Almost persuaded," Christ to receive;
Seems now some soul to say,
"Go, Spirit, Go Thy Way,
Some more convenient day,
On Thee I'll call"

"Almost persuaded," come, come today;
"Almost persuaded," turn not away;
Jesus invites you here
Angels are ling'ring near
Prayers rise from hearts so dear;
O wand'rer, come!

"Almost persuaded," harvest is past!
"Almost persuaded," doom comes at last!
"Almost" cannot avail;
"Almost" is but to fail!
Sad, sad, that bitter wail –
"Almost," but lost!

    The church grew both spiritually and numerically. The majority of the mill village families became members. Young people reached out to others who had not yet been "saved". Saturday night prayer meetings were held in homes and others were invited to attend.

    My two brothers, Paul and Leon, were not Christians yet. As described earlier, they had fun on weekends and kept a bottle of whisky in the back pocket of their overalls. Otha and Mattie invited them to a fried chicken supper before prayer meeting. Clinton Sheehan was the preacher. Before going into Otha's house, they hid their whisky bottles in the shrubbery. That night both my brothers got saved.

    Several years later, during a revival meeting and at the age of twelve, I walked down and knelt at the altar, a bench placed near the communion table.

By now John W. Ballard was pastor. He was a highly capable and loving shepherd.

An older sister and Pastor Ballard knelt beside me and prayed. Then we stood as Pastor Ballard presented me to the church for baptism and membership. It was not an emotional experience but rather a feeling that a heavy burden had been lifted, accompanied by a feeling of deep peace.

In later years I was given notes from a couple of the sermons that Pastor Ballard preached. I still have these notes among my personal papers, providing a glimpse into the manner of preaching in Baptist churches in the American South at the time. The sermon was based on the Old Testament story of Jonah and the whale:

It cost several dollars to get away from God and it cost three days and three nights in the belly of the great fish to get back.

The price of an automobile has gotten many away from God, they had to come back from a hospital cot, all broken and maimed for life.

The price of a movie has carried many of our young people away from God, they came back through the prison bars a criminal.

The price of a bottle of whisky has carried lots of people away from God, they came back broke, friends gone, an out-cast.

Let me say to you this day – you pay when you go away and you pay when you come back and how great is the price.

Southern Baptist churches nurture and disciple their members. The "mother church" on Vineville Avenue and its "mission church" in the mill village were similarly organized. The literature for Sunday School for both churches was the same. So was all the other literature written, printed and distributed by the denomination's publishing house. All of it stressed faith in Christ and commitment to world missions.

After Pastor Ballard left Willingham Baptist Church, other pastors were appointed for brief periods of time. Then Y.Z. Gordy, a young pastor, arrived. He had studied at Columbia Bible College in South Carolina. Foreign missions were emphasized at this school and a large percentage of its graduates went on to become missionaries.

Pastor Gordy often illustrated his sermons with missionary stories. As mentioned earlier, his library contained numerous missionary biographies including William Carey of India, Adoniram and Anne Judson of Burma, David Livingston of Africa and Jonathan Goforth of China. I read all of them as a high school student and was inspired by them.

At age fifteen I wondered what God's plan would be for my own life. Through Pastor Gordy's ministry, I became convinced that God was calling me to spend my life on the foreign mission field. I thought and prayed a lot about it and one day I went into the woods and knelt beneath a pine tree not far from where I now live. There I accepted what I believe was God's call for my life.

After graduating from Sidney Lanier High School in 1947, I applied for and was accepted at Columbia Bible College in Columbia, South Carolina. I still remember when the college catalog arrived. I sat on the porch of our house on Ben Hill Drive and read through it. I knew immediately that this was where I would go to school, though perhaps not fully realizing at the time just how much my life would be changed by my experience there.

Pastor Gordy had studied at Columbia Bible College for one year. Papa had a second grade education. Together the two of them drove me to Columbia later that year, leaving me there to begin a totally new life.

I loved my time at Columbia in almost every way. Still, my financial situation was almost always precarious. I worked in the college dining room but it still was not enough. I almost had to drop out of college for lack of funds.

Then a note arrived from Dean Munro, unexpectedly providing me with $100. It was a gift from Dr. and Mrs. Baldwin, a friend of Columbia Bible College, who lived on Weldon Drive in Chattanooga, Tennessee. One hundred dollars went a long way in 1949 and it was enough to ensure that I could continue and eventually complete my college education

After completing my four years at Columbia Bible College I enrolled at New Orleans Theological Seminary. Bettie registered as a nursing student at the nearby Baptist Hospital Nursing School whose students also studied at Tulane University.

I proposed to Bettie outside the Baptist Hospital on Napolean Avenue, underneath the oak trees draped with Spanish moss. Earlier that evening we had milkshakes at a nearby drugstore. We then walked down St. Charles Avenue hand-in-hand.

Not knowing what to do, we passed by the Touro Synagogue and saw people walking in to attend the Yom Kippur services there. We decided to attend as well. We were warmly welcomed and watched the service from the balcony.

Bettie decided to withdraw from training as a nurse. She returned to Macon to plan our wedding, set for June 19, 1953 at Mikado Baptist Church on Mikado Avenue in Macon. Our pastor Dr. E.C. Sheehan conducted the ceremony. Don Van Hoozier, well known as a musician in Macon at the time, played the piano. Church music director Gene Payne sang two songs, *Always* and *To Do Thy Will*.

Papa and Mama attended our wedding and my brother Leon was Best Man. Archie Davis, my Columbia Bible College roomate and life-long friend, also attended. I had been Best Man in his wedding in Atlanta earlier. He had married another Columbia Bible College classmate, Jane Powell. He devoted his life to the Presbyterian ministry and was pastor at churches in Florida, Georgia and South Carolina.

Sixty-five years after our wedding, on June 19, 2018, I wrote this love letter to Bettie as a token and appreciation for the life we forged together:

Sixty-five years together. It has been a marvelous journey -- a journey beyond our craziest imagination when we started out. I want you to know that every day of our life together I have thanked God for you. You kept me on course and I shudder to think what would have happened to me were you not on my side these 23,725 days.

I know that I have not been as great a husband for you as you have been as great a wife for me. I thank God that you have been forgiving.

You have made a beautiful home for us wherever we have lived. You have served nutritious meals on lovely table settings. You have been a gracious host to countless guests. We have served the Lord together both in America and in Pakistan. We have been partners in ministry. You have been a loving mother to our children. On and on I could go in praise and appreciation. I have been blest beyond measure to have walked these 65 years with you.

I spent three years at New Orleans Seminary, one of them as a married student living in married housing. The first two years were in the Garden District off St. Charles Avenue at the old campus seminary. For the final year, we lived on the new campus on Dement Street in Gentilly.

I thrived both inside and outside the classroom during my time in New Orleans. Extracurricular activities included service as a summer student missionary, first in Russellville in the Arkansas Ozarks and later in Cimmeron and Dodge City in western Kansas.

In addition, I joined fellow seminary students almost every Sunday in holding gospel services in towns along the bayous toward Grand Isle, providing exposure to yet another

American sub-culture, this one the Catholic Cajun culture of coastal Louisiana with its French-speaking roots.

I graduated from New Orleans Seminary in May 1954. Looking at the graduation program all these years later, I see that the music arranged for this week filled with special events at John Bunyan Chapel included *Lead on O King Eternal, I Sought the Lord, Guide Me O Thou Great Jehovah* and *Love Divine, All Love Excelling*. My New Orleans education had introduced me to many outstanding professors, giving me a good grounding in theology that would stay with me for the rest of my life.

Shortly thereafter Bettie and I were appointed as missionaries to Pakistan under the Conservative Baptist Foreign Mission Society (CBFMS), based at the time in Chicago and drawing most of its support from churches outside the southern United States.

In retrospect, the decision to become a missionary was the seemingly inevitable next step in a spiritual journey that had started as a child on Ben Hill Drive during the Great Depression, a journey that would eventually take me literally to the ends of the earth.

Chapter Five
Pakistan

Looking back, the road from Ben Hill Drive to a lifetime of missionary service spent largely in Pakistan seems unlikely and at times even unbelievable. Growing up on a farm in rural Middle Georgia, it was hard to imagine where this road might eventually lead.

After graduating from Columbia Bible College (now Columbia International University), I attended New Orleans Theological Seminary in Louisiana. Meanwhile, Bettie embarked on her own faith journey, attending Tennessee Temple College in Chattanooga and starting nurses training, also in New Orleans. When we married in Macon on June 19, 1953, we had already dedicated ourselves to a calling that would involve foreign missions.

Three years later Bettie and I left by ship for Pakistan under the auspices of the Conservative Baptist Foreign Mission Society. We were in our mid twenties. Our oldest son David was eighteen months old and accompanied us.

The three of us boarded a Liberty World War II era cargo ship in New York harbor. It was called the *Steel King*. We crossed the Atlantic Ocean and the Mediterranean Sea to Beirut, then sailed through the Suez Canal and across the Red Sea into the Arabian Sea and the Indian Ocean. We finally arrived at the port of Karachi. We had been on the ship for five weeks.

Pakistan is a large country, about the size of Texas and Oklahoma combined. It now has a population of more than 200 million people though when we first arrived in 1956 the population was more on the order of 60 million. It is situated between India and Afghanistan with a short border with China to the north. When we first arrived, it had been independent for less than ten years. The British colonial influence at that time was still quite strong.

We settled in a small town named Ratodero in the southern province of Sindh, one of Pakistan's four provinces. During our more than thirty years in Pakistan, we lived in several other cities and towns throughout Sindh province which is roughly the size of the state of Georgia. Those towns included Shikarpur, Hyderabad and Karachi, the largest city in the country.

After four years years we had our first "furlough," bringing with us two more children, Jonathan and Nancy, born in the northern town of Murree, nestled in the foothills of the Himalayas. During those early years we lived in Murree during the summer months, taking language lessons in both Sindhi and Urdu.

One purpose of furlough was to report back to the churches that had supported us. In one of the first churches we spoke in, I started by saying, "For the past four years, I have been living in Sindh. Let me tell you about it". That got everyone's attention. I have to be careful to pronounce the "D" at the end of the word "Sindh".

Most of our various ministries during the 34 years that we lived and worked in Pakistan involved team work with fellow missionaries and Pakistani nationals. Each area of emphasis involves a fascinating story, a story that continued long after we left and goes on to this day. Some of our many and varied areas of involvement included:

1. Launching and conducting the Pakistan Bible Correspondence School for Sindhi-speaking Muslims. This work continues after more than sixty years.

2. Finding and purchasing land, in turn leading to the establishment and building of a women's hospital in Shikarpur. Opened in the mid 1960s, the hospital is greatly appreciated for its work in responding to complicated cases for which medical services might otherwise not be available. Over the years the female doctors working there have delivered thousands of babies, often by C-Section. In 2019 the hospital marked the fiftieth anniversary of its founding.

3. Translating and publishing the New Testament into common language Sindhi. This is now the standard New Testament among the Sindhi people.

4. Producing a basic Sindhi language learning course for English speakers. We had no textbook to guide us in learning Sindhi when we first arrived. We had to learn by simply listening to Sindhis talk. After I became literate in the Sindhi language, fellow missionary Polly Brown joined me in producing a course for newcomers.

5. Training and equipping Pakistani pastors and other church leaders to become more effective.

6. Starting and pastoring the International Church of Karachi that met first in our home and then in a local hotel.

7. Providing initial support for what later became a mass movement for Christ among a tribe of outcaste Hindus.

These and other aspects of our work are described from Bettie's point of view in her book *The Day the Chicken Cackled: Reflections on a Life in Pakistan* (Bloomington, IN: Crossbooks, 2009). Our second son Jonathan also provided his perspective as the child of missionaries serving in Pakistan in his memoir *Some Far and Distant Place* (Athens, GA: University of Georgia

Press, 1997). The Sindhi language course I helped develop has also been published under the title *Sindhi: An Introductory Course for English Speakers* (Doorlight Publications, 2010).

Looking back, one area of ministry that seems worth highlighting and has been rarely covered elsewhere is our intriguing work among an "outcaste" Hindu group living in Sindh province, large numbers of whom have become Christians over the past half century.

Pakistan is an Islamic Republic and approximately 97 percent of the population is considered Muslim. This includes both Sunni and Shia Muslims along with other, smaller Muslim populations such as the Ismailis. Most of my work involved bearing witness among Pakistan's Muslim population.

We did work among Pakistan's Christian minority as well, representing about 1.5 percent of Pakistan's population and now numbering more than three million. Most of these Pakistani Christians live in Punjab province but they are also represented in large numbers in Karachi and in smaller numbers in most other cities and provincial towns across the country including Shikarpur.

Pakistan's Hindu population represents another 1.5 percent of the country's population and are concentrated mainly in Sindh province. Most of Pakistan's urban Hindu population departed for India as refugees when the country was established in 1947, even as many Muslims living in certain parts of India left for Pakistan. Many of those Hindus who remained in Pakistan were considered "outcastes," coming as they did from marginal and impoverished tribal populations that were often despised by the rest of population, both Muslim and Hindu.

The Hindu tribal people who stayed in Pakistan after independence were typically known by their occupation. For example, one tribe digs irrigation ditches, another makes baskets, a third is employed as sanitation workers. The ones that we came to know earned their livelihood from harvesting the fields of wealthy Muslim landlords, often travelling from place to place in response to the agricultural calendar.

We were always aware of this community as they walked along the roads of Sindh province. They live in small villages in houses made of mud and thatched roofs. The women wore brightly colored full skirts with lots of bangles on their arms. They spoke their own language and kept largely to themselves. We often wondered how we could get to know them.

We had been in Pakistan for about six years when it happened. A man rang our door bell. I opened the door and he introduced himself in Sindhi. He told me that he was a Hindu from a village about sixty miles north. His name was Domji.

According to Domji, he had been walking along the road north of Sukkur when he picked up a piece of paper. It was an application to study the Bible in Sindhi by correspondence. Domji was literate in Sindhi and had applied.

He received our course called The Way of Salvation, based on the familiar passage in John 3:16. He told me that he had come to know Jesus and wanted me to come to his village and help him tell his family and village about it.

Domji was from a tribe of Hindus known as the "Marwaris". He said that there were many thousands of Marwaris all over Sindh and that if I would come with him together we could preach and they too would believe in Jesus. I promised to come. He gave me directions to his village and a Pakistani evangelist named Ghulam Masih ("Servant of Christ") accompanied me.

The journey took more than an hour. When we got there, Domji had gathered the entire village and they sat on the ground as Ghulam and I talked to them.

Domji asked us to baptize him and his people. I replied that I wanted to provide more teaching first. He invited my family to come and stay in his village and teach them. The women wanted very much for me to bring my wife and children. We set a date and Bettie, Nancy and I went prepared to stay for one week. David and Jonathan were at this time 800 miles to the north, attending boarding school in Murree. Nancy, our youngest, was not yet in first grade and was still living with us in Shikarpur.

The day came and we loaded our Land Rover for the trip north to Domji's village. We took our tent, sleeping bags, portable kerosene stove, groceries, bottled water and aspirin. We planned to camp near Domji's house so we wouldn't be a burden.

When we arrived, we were warmly welcomed by people from the village. After this initial welcome, it was time to settle in. When we told Domji that we planned to camp out on our own, he firmly objected. He took me aside and said this to me: "Mr. Addleton, if you live separately from us, the people here will think that you don't accept us and that you are like the Muslims who surround us and despise us."

Then he showed us the house he had prepared for us. It was in the middle of the village, a small mud house like all the other ones. Inside were two rope-strung beds. A family had vacated it and would sleep outside during our stay.

Domji also walked us outside the village a short way, showing us the toilet he had made for us. The villagers at that time didn't use toilets, rather they simply walked out of sight to the fields and shrubs nearby.

He knew that wouldn't do for Bettie and Nancy. So he had dug a hole in the ground and placed two planks over it, leaving a little space between them. He had also placed a large straw mat in a circle around the hole to provide some measure of privacy, serving as his version of a latrine.

Domji and the villagers had gone to great efforts to make our stay comfortable. We were concerned that we would be a burden but they seemed to feel pride and honor in hosting us. Of course, we gave ourselves to their hospitality and lived as they live for the week.

When we finally lay down to sleep in our hut that first night, it seemed as if the entire village filed passed our beds to view us. Now I know what it is like to "lie in state"! We were the first foreigners to enter their village and be their guests.

During the night I was briefly awakened by the sound of a dog knocking a bucket over outside. Bettie was awakened by a possible insect bite. She asked me if I thought we could live here for a week. Nancy slept soundly and we too tried to sleep.

Domji's wife cooked delicious curries and Bettie still uses one of her recipes. The village women talked incessantly with her. Nancy played with Domji's daughter all day. They were about the same age. In the evening Domji and I drove to several surrounding villages and showed filmstrips related to the life and message of Jesus.

Domji asked me to baptize him as well as other members of his community. Again, I told him that we would plan for that only after more teaching. In Pakistan, conversion is a complicated and at times controversial process. For a Muslim, it might mean cutting themselves off from family, persecution or even death. For a Hindu, it might not mean much other than the addition of another object of veneration to their pantheon of already existing gods. Returning to Shikarpur, I was so busy that I kept putting off driving back to Domji's village for a return visit.

Early one morning I heard the doorbell ring. I got up and walked sleepily across the courtyard in my pajamas, opening the wooden door leading out into the street. A small group of people was standing there – Domji, his wife, his two young sons and two other young men.

Domji said, "Mr. Addleton, you said you would baptize us when you give us more teaching; you haven't come so we have come to stay with you so you can teach us and baptize us".

Each of our early morning visitors were carrying a bedroll. I knew then that Domji was serious and I could not turn them away.

I welcomed our unexpected guests inside to sit down. Bettie got out of bed and prepared tea while I thought about what to do next. Down the street was an empty house belonging to a missionary family on furlough. We invited Domji and his family and friends to stay there. They were very happy with the arrangement.

I also sent a telegram to a Sindhi evangelist named Benjamin Dean to come and help me teach. Benjamin was a former Muslim and a wonderful co-worker who lived in another town. He came immediately and after three days of teaching both Benjamin and I knew that they were ready. We loaded everyone into our two Land Rovers and drove a mile down the road to a nearby irrigation canal where we baptized them.

All through the following year Domji educated me about himself and his people. He was a Hindu and often went on pilgrimage to Hindu shrines with their myriad gods embodied in various forms. He himself had carved an idol of his own out of a piece of wood, placing it in a small mud hut as a kind of personal shrine. He worshipped before it and one day he noticed that the termites were eating it. This episode with the termites convinced him – if the termites were stronger than his god, he would no longer worship it.

He became miserable and launched his search for the true God. He first began by looking into other branches of Hinduism, travelling to some of the well-known Hindu shrines of India. He also thought about converting to Islam, as some of the outcaste Hindus around him were doing. None of these efforts brought the peace of mind that he was looking for.

He went to a Catholic church and talked with a priest. He was attracted to Jesus and his teachings but was put off by the statues in the church. Then he found the piece of paper along the road which was the application to study the Bible through the Pakistan Bible Correspondence School.

Completely unexpectedly, Domji's conversion during the 1960s helped ignite what became a mass movement toward Christianity among this outcaste Hindu tribe. More than half a century later, the number of Christians from Domji's tribe reaches into the thousands and Marwari Christians meet in dozens of house churches up and down the Indus River.

The world has changed drastically since those years in the 1950s, 1960s and 1970s when we worked in Pakistan as missionaries. The work among the Marwari tribe was only one part of a larger ministry that encompassed a variety of efforts aimed at strengthening the Pakistani church and bearing witness among the majority Muslim community that surrounded it.

There are now fewer missionaries from Europe and United States in Pakistan than was the case during our time there. But the work continues, led in large part by Pakistani Christians facing many challenges. But foreign churchworkers also remain involved, including some from other countries including Canada, Korea and Ethiopia.

We departed Pakistan in 1976 as our three children entered college and began making lives of their own. David, Jonathan and Nancy each married and each had families of their own. They in turn have given us our several grandchildren, all of whom are now young adults – Adriana, Alexandra, John, Iain, Cameron and Catriona; David has a stepson as well, also called Ian.

Bettie and I reconnected with our families, most still living in Macon but some living as far afield as New Hampshire and Colorado. I served as a pastor at Southside Baptist Church in Cochran, GA for several years before making the decision to return to Pakistan for a second time, this time under the Southern Baptist Foreign Mission Board. Reconnecting with fellow missionaries as well as Pakistani Christians, we served in Pakistan for another ten years.

Bettie and I formally retired as missionaries in 1995, when I turned sixtyfive. I once again became a pastor, serving for many years at Antioch Baptist Church in Taylor County, a small country church with a long history going back to the early 1800s when it was the first Baptist church in Georgia established west of the Flint River. I continued to serve as pastor to the small congregation at Antioch until 2009 when I reached the age of eighty.

Once again we returned to our roots. And once again we returned to Ben Hill Drive. There are now eight houses on the hill, occupying spaces where I once herded cows on the Addleton farm.

Of these eight houses, seven were once owned by Addletons. The eighth house, what I still call the Stevens House, named after the original owners, has been bought and sold several times; it is located on a beautiful 16-acre property with pine trees and a small fishing pond but the house itself is in need of significant renovation.

Three other houses on Ben Hill Drive, originally built by Addletons, are no longer in the family. This includes the red brick house across the street from the Stevens House, originally built by my brother Otha. It later had two other owners, first the Bush couple and then Curtis James and his wife who still live there to this day.

The wooden house built near the top of the hill by my sister Velma and her husband William was also sold outside the family, as was an adjacent house built by her daughter and now owned by a "blended" family from Florida with seven children. It is gratifying to see another generation of young children swim in Walnut Creek and explore the woods nearby. The children next door also sometimes join us to make puzzles or play scrabble.

Four other houses on Ben Hill Drive remain in the Addleton family, at least for now. One is occupied by Bennie, Louise's youngest son. Another is owned by my niece and rented out. My brother B.L. and his wife Betty Anne live in a third, just across the street from us, visited often by their children, grandchildren and now great children.

Sometimes my mind wanders back to the 1930s, when I was a child growing up on Ben Hill Drive and the place where I live was still pastureland.

It is hard to believe that my oldest sibling was born in 1912, prior to the start of World War I. He was less than fifty years removed from the Civil War, the conflict that shaped so much of the South in which I was raised. When he started his life, airplanes were still a novelty; by the end of it, man had walked on the moon.

Now my grandchildren are part of a very different age, as distant in time from the Vietnam War as my oldest brother was from the Civil War when he was born. No doubt there will be many dramatic changes in the years ahead, changes that we can hardly begin to fathom.

Bettie and I now live in an apartment in the basement of the last house on Ben Hill Drive, marking the end of our dead-end street. We are situated within the Macon city limits but beyond us there is only forest. After decades of living on the other side of the world, we have come home.

Grandpa Robert E. Addleton, early 1900s

Grandpa John Wesley Gordon, early 1900s

Papa and Mama as I remember them

Bettie, early 1950s; this is the photo I kept on my desk at New Orleans Seminary before we married in 1953

Another photo of Bettie

The two of us during the 1950s

Another photo of the two of us

Hubert with school friends during the 1930s in Jones County Hubert is on the bottom right in overalls; Bettie's brother James Simmons, a good friend, is standing directly behind him.

Three of the younger Addleton siblings during the 1930s
Gloria, BL and Hubert

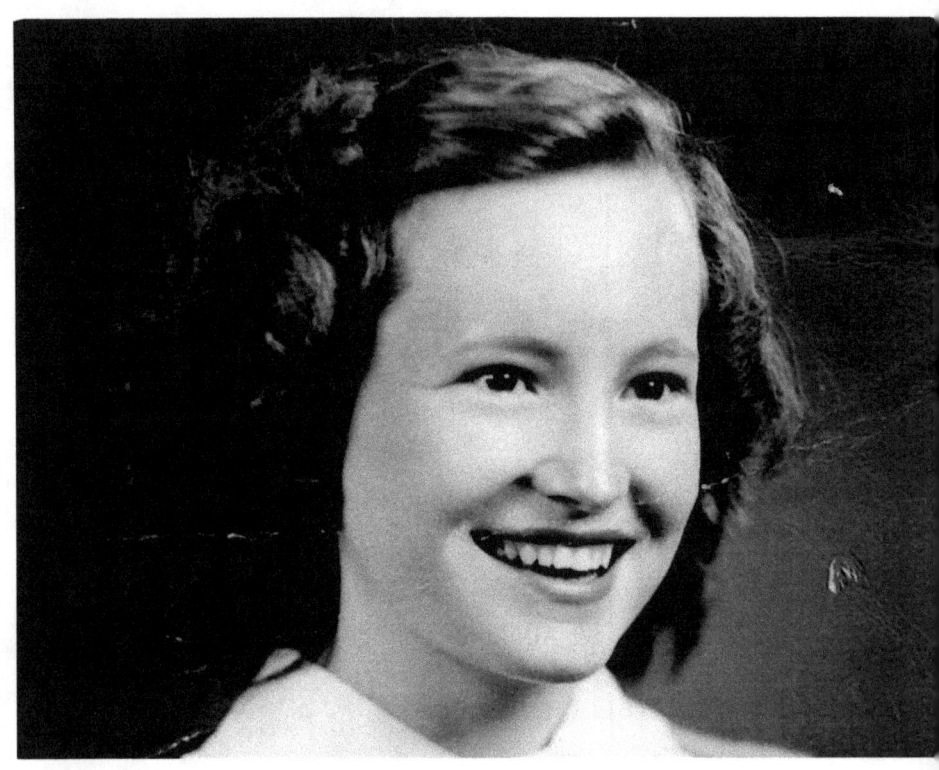

Bettie at 16

Hubert at 16

Hubert near Old Clinton Road in Macon, early 1940s

Hubert on horseback while serving as a summer missionary in Arkansas, early 1950s

Hubert at a country church in the Ozarks where he served as a summer missionary, early 1950s

Hubert standing with local kids beside a vintage car while serving as a summer missionary in Arkansas, early 1950s

Hubert and Bettie on their wedding day at Mikado Baptist Church in Macon on June 19, 1953

Bettie as a beautiful bride

Cutting the cake

Mama, Papa, Bettie's mother, and Bettie's youngest sister Mary Frances at our wedding.

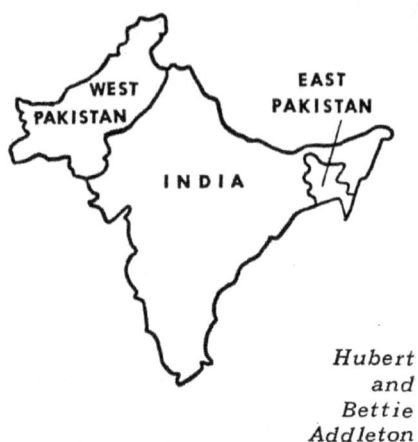

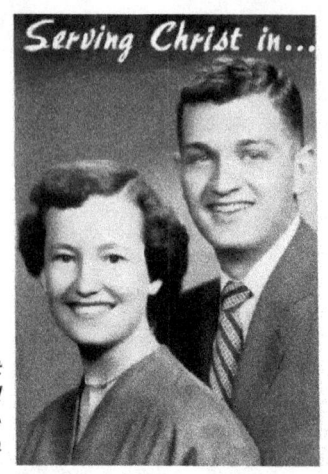

"Ye also helping us together by prayer...
—II Cor. 1:11
". . . to preach the gospel, not where Christ was named...
—Rom. 15:20
"For we are labourers together with God."
—I Cor. 3:9
WEST PAKISTAN
EAST PAKISTAN
INDIA
Hubert and Bettie Addleton
Serving Christ in...

First "prayer card" issued by CBFMS after our appointment as prospective missionaries to Pakistan in 1954

Domji's baptism in a canal outside Shikarpur (Sindh), 1960s

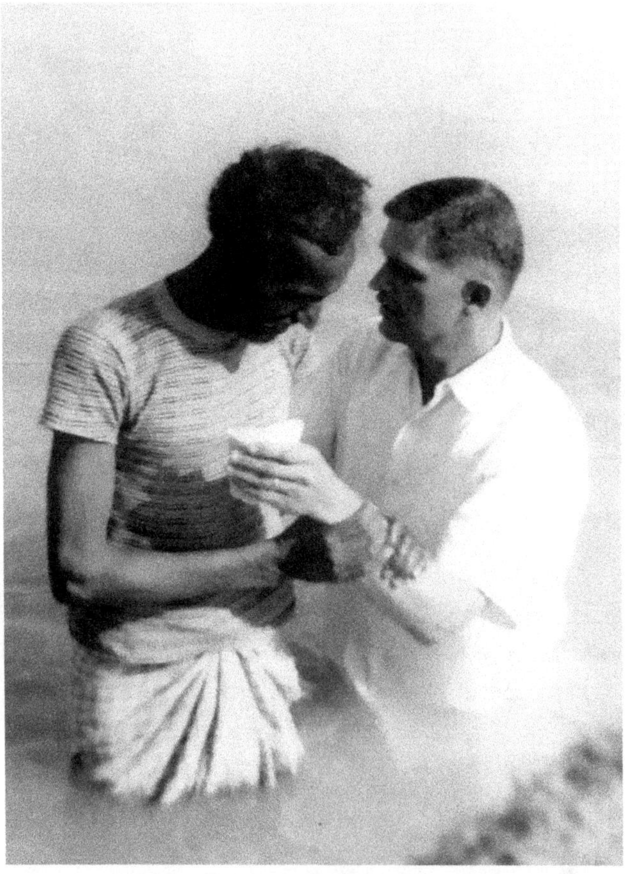

Bettie, David and I in Mama and Papa's home in Macon, shortly before our departure for Pakistan in 1956

Family photo with David and Jonathan before Nancy was born, taken in Pakistan late 1950s

Family photo at David's graduation in Murree, 1973

Family photo with Jonathan and Nancy after David left following his high school graduation, Pakistan 1974

Depression Era photo outside our house on Second Street, Macon, 1930s
Back Row, Left to Right: Otha, James, Paul, Leon, John
Front Row, Left to Right: Papa, Hilda, Velma, Louise, Annie Ruth, Hubert on Mama's knee

Depression Era photo outside our shack on Graham Road, 1930s
Back Row, Left to Right: Otha, John, James, Leon, Paul
Middle Row, Left to Right: Hilda, Velma, Louise, Papa, Mama
Front Row, Left to Right: Gloria, Helen, Johnny (nephew), BL, Hubert

Post World War II Family photo, Ben Hill Drive, 1950s
Back Row, Left to Right: Hubert, Louise, Papa, Velma, BL
Middle Row, Left to Right: Leon, Helen, Hilda, Mama, Annie Ruth, Gloria
Front Row, Left to Right: Otha, James, John, Paul

Post World War II family photo, 1950s
Back Row, Left to Right: Velma, Annie Ruth, Gloria, Paul, BL, Otha, Hilda
Middle Row, Left to Right: Louise, Papa, Mama, Helen
Front Row, Left to Right: Leon, James, John, Hubert

Post World War II family photo, 1950s
Standing, Left to Right: Helen, James, Paul, John, Papa, Hubert, Leon, Otha, Gloria, BL
Sitting, Left to Right: Annie Ruth, Louise, Mama, Velma, Hilda

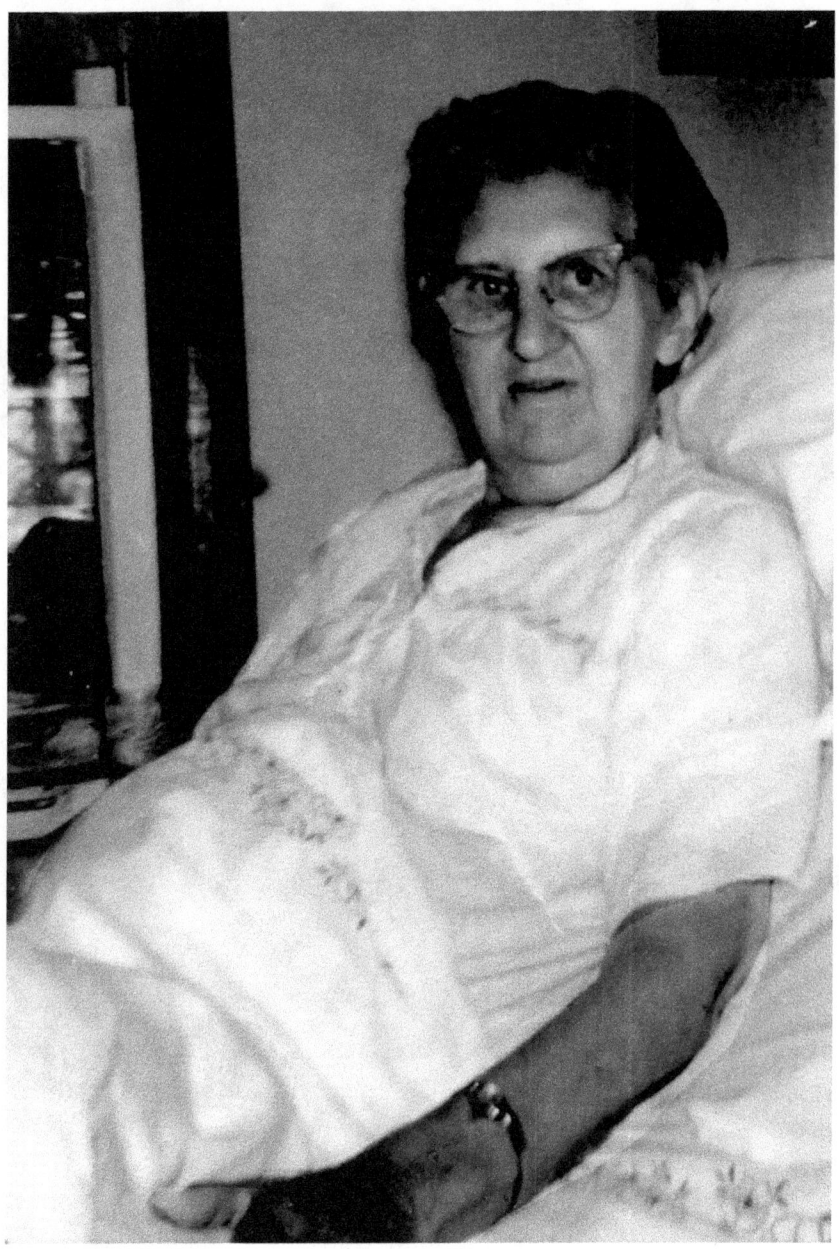

Last photograph of Mama, taken by Jonathan in 1965 just before returning to Pakistan

50th Anniversary Photo at Fontana Village in North Carolina where we spent our honeymoon:
Back Row, Left to Right: Jeff, Nancy, Fiona, Jonathan, Bettie, Hubert, David, Alexandra (Alec), Adriana
Front Row, Left to Right: John, Catriona, Cameron, Iain

Acknowledgments

Special thanks to Daniel Brown and Ruth Anne Burke from Doorlight Publications for turning this manuscript into a book.

Our children David, Jonathan and Nancy also helped in various ways, with Jonathan writing the forword and assisting with editing while David and Nancy helped with photographs. David's detailed research into the Addleton family tree also proved helpful in finalizing this book.

Special thanks to Betty Anne Addleton, wife of my brother B.L. who has always taken an interest in Addleton family history and has lived on Ben Hill Drive for many decades. She also provided useful anecdotes about the Addleton family, several of which are included in the text of this manuscript.

Finally, my wife Bettie helped pave the way for this book by writing her own memoir that includes much greater detail on our life in Pakistan, *The Day the Chicken Cackled* (Crossbooks, 2009). She also read this manuscript and made a number of useful suggestions as it moved toward completion.

Appendix A
Education History

Jones County Grammar School
Gray, GA

Alexander III Grammar School
Macon, GA

Sidney Lanier High School for Boys
Macon, GA
(High School Diploma)

Columbia Bible College
Columbia, SC
(Bachelor of Arts in Biblical Education)

New Orleans Baptist Theological Seminary
New Orleans, LA
(Masters in Theology)

University of Toronto
Toronto, Ontario, Canada
(Short course in Linguistics)

Hartford Seminary
Hartford, CN
(Post-Graduate Semester in Islamics)

University of Chicago
Chicago, IL
(Post-Graduate Semester in Linguistics)

Appendix B
Pastorates

O'Zion Baptist Church
Meadville, MS
(1953-1954)

Houston Heights Baptist Church
Macon, GA
(1954-1955)*

Southside Baptist Church
Cochran, GA
(1978-1984)

International Church of Karachi
Karachi, Pakistan
(1987-1994)

Friendship Baptist Church
Milledgeville, GA
(1995)*

Hillcrest Baptist Church
Columbus, GA
(1995-1996)*

Antioch Baptist Church
Butler, GA
(1996-2010)

*Interim Pastorate

Appendix C
Work History

Goins Grocery on Holt Avenue
Macon, GA ("The store stocked a cart of soft drinks, snack stuff and headache powders. I and Bubba Greenway wheeled it up the street into the Willingham Cotton Mill for the workers who called the cart the 'Dope Box'")

Uncle Horace's Hamburger Stand
Macon, GA ("End of bus line on Bellevue Avenue")
Hamburger flipper

Willingham Cotton Mill
Macon, GA
Carder

Herbert Smart Airport
Macon, GA
Airplane painter

Kenney's Shoes
Macon, GA
Salesman

Ben Lippen Camp
North Carolina
Camp Counselor

Southern Baptist Home Mission Board
Arkansas
Kansas
Student Missionary

Woolworth's
New Orleans, LA
Salesman ("Successful at selling stones that when taken home would grow grass")

Sears
New Orleans, LA and Macon, GA
Credit department clerk

Conservative Baptist Foreign Missionary Society
Wheaton, IL
Missionary to Pakistan, 1954-1978

International Mission Board
Richmond, VA
Missionary to Pakistan, 1985-1995

Bibb County School System
Macon, GA
Substitute Teacher

Smith and Helwys Publishing Company
Macon, GA
Book order department clerk, 1995-1996

Appendix D
Countries Visited

Afghanistan
Bangladesh
Belgium
Canada
China
England
Egypt
France
Germany
Greece
Guatemala
Hong Kong
India
Iran
Israel
Italy
Jordan
Kazakhstan
Kyrgyzstan

Lebanon
Luxembourg
Mongolia
Nepal
Netherlands
Pakistan
Philippines
Saudi Arabia
Scotland
South Africa
Spain
Switzerland
Syria
Thailand
Turkey
United States
Yemen
Zimbabwe

Appendix E
Genealogy

Children

David Franklin Addleton
Born in Macon, GA – December 30, 1954
Married Liv Nilssen (div)
Married Pam Shepard Cope – December 10, 2011

Jonathan Stuart Addleton
Born in Murree, Pakistan – June 27, 1957
Married Fiona Riach – August 17, 1985

Nancy Elizabeth Addleton
Born in Murree, Pakistan – July 5, 1959
Married Jeff White – July 12, 1991

Grandchildren

David's Children
Adriana Addleton (Born in Chicago, IL -- March 16, 1984)
Alexandra Addleton (Born in Atlanta, GA -- September 3, 1986)
Ian Cope (Stepson; son of Pam Cope; Born in Winston-Salem, NC – August 29, 1994)

Jonathan's Children:
Iain Addleton (Born in Inverness, Scotland – November 27, 1990)
Cameron Addleton (Born in Pretoria, South Africa – August 31, 1992)

Catriona Addleton (Born in Macon, Georgia – November 2, 1994)

Nancy's Children
John White (Born in Macon, GA – July 27, 1993)

Siblings

John Forest Addleton
Born in Bibb County, GA -- February 19, 1912
Died in Bibb County, GA -- March 13, 1974
Married Frances Hudson – June 24, 1933 (div)
Married Bessie Rogers
One son (Johnny), one daughter (Darlene)

Bennie Otha Addleton
Born in Houston County, GA – October 6, 1913
Died in Jones County, GA – July 17, 2005
Buried Evergreen Cemetery in Bibb County, Georgia
Married Mattie Stevens – October 6, 1934
One daughter (Diane)

James Edward Addleton
Born in Bibb County, GA November 9, 1915
Died in Sanford, FL –April 1983
Married Lillian Black – December 23, 1936 (div)
Married Florine Adams Prosser – February 20, 1956
One son (Ted) and two daughters (Jerry and Pam)

Annie Ruth Addleton
Born in Bibb County, GA – November 29, 1917
Died in Bibb County, GA – September 25, 1996
Married Cecil Ezekiel Cranford ("Buddy") – September 21, 1935
Buried Middle Georgia Memorial Gardens
One son (Eric), one daughter (Ellen)

Andrew Paul Addleton
Born in Bibb County, GA – September 10, 1919
Died in Bibb County, GA – August 3, 2009
Married Mary Davis – June 5, 1942
One daughter (Paulette)

William Leon Addleton
Born in Bibb County, GA – August 30, 1920
Died in North Carolina – July 15, 1999
Married Hilda Glass – July 5, 1941
Buried in Evergeen Cemetery in Bibb County, GA
One son (Larry), one daughter (Marveen)

Louise Bessie Addleton
Born in Bibb County, GA – June 28, 1923
Died in Bibb County, GA – November 29, 2010
Married Robert Henry Duffey, Jr. – April 29, 1956
Buried in Middle Georgia Memorial Gardens
Two sons (Tim and Bennie)

Velma Addleton
Born in Jones County, GA – November 12, 1924
Died in Bibb County, GA – September 7, 2004
Married William Lewis Whitehead – July 26, 1941
Buried in Macon Memorial Park
Three daughters (Carol, Jeanette, Gena)

Hilda Nevada Addleton
Born September 18, 1926
Died October 28, 2014
Married Buck Mixon – May 9, 1947
Buried in Macon Memorial Park
One son (Ricky), one daughter (Renee)

Claude Robert Addleton
Born May 30, 1928
Died February 12, 1929
Buried Shiloh Primitive Baptist Church, Old Columbus Road, Macon, GA

Helen Addleton
Born in Bibb County, GA – March 27, 1931
Married James Henry Tucker – April 8, 1950
One son (Mike), two daughters (Janet and Judy)

Gloria Mae Addleton
Born September 9, 1932
Died October 27, 1975
Married Julius Haskins ("Dude") – July 29, 1950
Buried Middle Georgia Memorial Gardens
Two sons (Andy and Lark)

Bob Lawrence ("BL") Addleton
Born in Bibb County, GA – November 6, 1933
Married Betty Anne Law – February 8, 1958
One son (Chris), one daughter (Robin)

Parents

Benjamin Lark Addleton
Born in Jones County, GA – May 22, 1888
Died in Bibb County, GA – October 13, 1982
Buried Middle Georgia Memorial Gardens

Bessie (Gordon) Addleton
Born in Crawford County, GA – November 19, 1894
Died in Bibb County, GA – June 25, 1966
Buried Middle Georgia Memorial Gardens

Grandparents (Mother's Side)

John Wesley Gordon
Born 1870 in Georgia
Died September 25, 1922 in Crawford County, GA

Anna Marshall
Born 1873 in Georgia
Died January 23, 1929 in Bibb County, GA

Grandparents (Father's Side)

Robert E. Addleton
Born 1854 in Georgia
Died April 9, 1928 in Bibb County, GA
Buried Shiloh Primitive Baptist Church Cemetery in Macon

Penelope ("Penny") Griffin
Born 1854 in Georgia
Date of death unknown

Note: *Robert E. Addleton was the son of Cyrus D. Addleton, born in Massachusetts in 1813; his mother was Eliza Kitchens, born in Georgia in 1829. Robert E. Addleton married twice. His first wife was Penny Griffin who was Papa's mother; she had two other sons, Park and Robert Lee who was called "Joe". His second wife was Mary Wilson and they had four children together — Sam, Horace, Eva and Lucille.*

About the Author

Hubert F. Addleton was born in Bibb County, GA on November 30, 1929. A graduate of Sidney Lanier High School in Macon, he has also studied at Columbia Bible College, New Orleans Seminary, Hartford Seminary and the University of Chicago.

Addleton served for 34 years as a missionary to Pakistan, first under the Conservative Baptist Foreign Mission Society and later under the Southern Baptist Foreign Mission Board. He has also pastored a number of churches including O'Zion Baptist Church in Meadville, Mississippi; Southside Baptist Church in Cochran, Georgia; and Antioch Baptist Church in Butler, Georgia.

While serving in Pakistan, he translated large parts of the New Testament into the Sindhi language. He also co-authored a Sindhi language textbook, *Sindhi: An Introductory Course for English Speakers* (Doorlight Publications, 2010).

Addleton is married to the former Bettie Rose Simmons who also grew up in Jones County, GA. They have three adult children, all of whom now live in Macon, GA: David, a consumer protection lawyer involved in cases across the state of Georgia; Jonathan, a retired US Ambassador who now teaches in the Department of International and Global Studies at Mercer University; and Nancy, a former member of the Macon City Council who now serves as Director of Operations for South Georgia Healthy Start, an initiative of the Mercer University School of Medicine.

www.ingramcontent.com/pod-product-compliance
Lightning Source LLC
Chambersburg PA
CBHW060200050426
42446CB00013B/2917